EBB AND FLOW

EBB AND FLOW

VOLUME 1. WATER, MIGRATION, AND DEVELOPMENT

Esha Zaveri, Jason Russ, Amjad Khan, Richard Damania,
Edoardo Borgomeo, and Anders Jägerskog

CONTENTS

BOXES

FIGURES

MAPS

TABLES

ACKNOWLEDGMENTS

This book was prepared by a World Bank team led by Esha Zaveri and comprising Jason Russ, Amjad Khan, Richard Damania, Edoardo Borgomeo, and Anders Jägerskog. Richard Damania (Chief Economist) led the team during the early stages of this work and continued to provide overall guidance. The book has greatly benefited from the strategic guidance and general direction of Juergen Voegele (Vice President, Sustainable Development Practice Group), Jennifer Sara (Global Director, Water Practice), Soma Ghosh Moulik (Practice Manager), Carmen Nonay (Practice Manager), and the management of the Water Global Practice.

In addition to research completed by the authors, this work draws on background papers, notes, and analysis, prepared by the following: Guy Abel (International Institute for Applied Systems Analysis-IIASA & Shanghai University), Remi Jedwab (George Washington University), Raya Muttarak (International Institute for Applied Systems Analysis-IIASA), and Fabian Stephany (University of Oxford).

The team greatly benefited from incisive and thoughtful comments and guidance from internal peer reviewers—Christian Borja-Vega (Senior Economist), Urmila Chatterjee (Senior Economist), Viviane Wei Chen Clement (Climate Change Specialist), Erwin De Nys (Lead Water Resources Management Specialist), Nathan Engle (Senior Climate Change Specialist), Nancy Lozano Gracia (Senior Economist), Somik Lall (Lead Urban Economist), Muthukumara Mani (Lead Economist), Dilip Ratha (Lead Economist), Dominick Revell de Waal (Senior Economist), Kanta Kumari Rigaud (Lead Environmental Specialist), Aude-Sophie Rodella (Senior Economist), Amal Talbi (Lead Water Resources Management Specialist), and Dorte Verner (Lead Agriculture Economist).

The team is also grateful to other colleagues from the World Bank for their helpful comments and suggestions at various stages of the book's development, including Nicolas Godoy (Consultant), Nora Kaoues (Program Manager), Sarah Keener (Senior Social Development Specialist), Mark R. Lundell (Regional Director), Hoveida Nobakht (Practice Manager), Ethel Sennhauser (Director), Sarah Simons (Senior Agriculture Specialist), Catherine Signe Tovey (Practice Manager), Martien Van Nieuwkoop (Global Director), Ioannis Vasileiou (Agriculture Economist), Pieter Waalewijn (Senior Water Resources Management Specialist), and Monika Weber-Fahr (Senior Manager).

The World Bank Water communications, knowledge, and publishing teams, particularly Erin Barrett, Meriem Gray, and Pascal Saura, provided valuable guidance for turning the manuscript into a finalized report. Eszter Bodnar provided excellent design support and designed several of the interior images. John Dawson provided excellent editorial support. Deborah Appel-Barker, Amy Lynn Grossman, Patricia Katayama, and Jewel McFadden from the World Bank's Publishing Program guided additional design, editing, and publication.

Finally, Georgine Badou provided helpful administrative support for which the team is grateful.

This work was made possible by the financial contribution of the Global Water Security and Sanitation Partnership (worldbank.org/gwsp) of the Water Global Practice, World Bank Group.

ABBREVIATIONS

APEX	Advanced Practices for Environmental Excellence in Cities
CSA	climate-smart agriculture
FAO	Food and Agricultural Organization of the United Nations
GDP	gross domestic product
GMDAC	Global Migration Data Analysis Centre
IATP	Institute for Agriculture and Trade Policy
IWGIA	International Work Group for Indigenous Affairs
MDG	mean decrease in Gini
OCHA	United Nations Office for the Coordination of Humanitarian Affairs
SD	standard deviation
SSP	socioeconomic pathways
UNDP	United Nations Development Programme
UNESCO	United Nations Educational, Scientific and Cultural Organization
UNHCR	United Nations High Commissioner for Refugees
UNOCHA	United Nations Office for the Coordination of Humanitarian Affairs

EXECUTIVE SUMMARY

What forces determine the movement of people, the transformation of economies, the wealth of nations? These age-old questions are the subject of a multitude of World Bank reports, academic papers, and enduring tomes because they are foundational to economic progress and the human condition. As the world's population careens toward 11 billion by the end of the century, the combination of demographic change, rising standards of living, and climate change will place increasing pressures on existing water resources. At the same time, the public health and economic fallout from the COVID-19 (coronavirus) pandemic is leading to large job losses and significant reduction of livelihoods, with dire consequences for those living in or near poverty. Against this backdrop, answering these questions will be imperative in the global fight to end poverty and achieve equitable and sustainable growth.

The increasing importance of mobility to local, regional, and global economies and to everyday life is reflected in data showing the relentless increase in the movement of people. Estimates suggest that there are currently over 1 billion migrants in the world, of which approximately three quarters are domestic migrants. These numbers are truly unprecedented, and yet as the world continues to become ever more interconnected and globalized, they will continue to climb and are likely even to accelerate. Migrants decide to move for many reasons. Some migrate for a chance to earn more and send back money to their family, or for a new employment or career opportunity; others migrate to avoid conflict, violence, or destruction from natural disasters. At the same time, many other would-be migrants may not move due to a variety of barriers that hold back migration; financial barriers, legal restrictions, and safety concerns may prevent many people from exploring new opportunities or attempting to escape a bad situation.

Exploring the relationship between water, migration, and development becomes all the more salient as climate change increasingly adds stresses to the water cycle. Increasing variability and uncertainty of rainfall can weigh heavily on communities and economies. Rainfall shocks, where precipitation is well below or above normal levels, are already becoming more frequent, and coping with them may present one of the most difficult challenges confronting humanity. These shocks lead to significant climate uncertainty that make investment decisions to promote adaptation difficult. For instance, by the end of the century, the likely change in rainfall in Africa could span anywhere from –4.3 percent to 65.4 percent depending on the chosen set of climate models, mitigation targets, and socioeconomic scenarios. The former outcome would call for investments for a drier future and the latter, a much wetter outcome. And indeed, in many areas extremes on both ends of the spectrum will become more frequent. This situation suggests the importance of no-regret policies that can buffer against rainfall extremes on the low end, the high end, and both simultaneously.

Climate variability exacerbated by climate change is expected to amplify and significantly affect existing patterns of migration. A recent World Bank report (Clement et al. 2021) estimates that slow-onset climate impacts due to climate change could lead up to 216 million people to become internal migrants. In regions such as Sub-Saharan Africa, this would imply additional migration representing more than 4 percent of the total population. With the vast majority of these migrants expected to end up in urban areas, cities must prepare to house and integrate them. Nevertheless, as shown in another World Bank report (Lall et al. 2021), most cities in developing countries are not prepared for efficient and sustainable expansion. Urban plans and planning institutions are often ineffective at coordinating development; urban land markets tend to be dysfunctional; and zoning and restrictive building regulations limit the size of structures, economic density, and ultimately urban efficiency.

The impacts of climate change are not some looming threat on the distant horizon—they are happening here and now. This report therefore looks back into the recent past to examine the role that droughts, floods, infrastructure, and other water-related factors have played in determining the movements of people. The analysis relies on empirical methods and big data to examine these relationships. Stepping back and letting the data speak for themselves allows for an evidence-based view of often sensitive and emotive issues. Understanding the triggers of migration and the resulting impacts on well-being and development is critical to finding the appropriate policy response. This report demonstrates that this understanding is especially important in the context of water and migration because there are differences in triggers and important nuances in the impacts of a given adverse "water event" that call for equally different policy responses.

Focus of the Report

Migration shapes the lives of those who move and transforms the geographies and economies of their points of departure and destinations alike. Although every migrant has a unique story, the decision to migrate can often be boiled down to two salient questions: Will I be better off in the long run if I choose to migrate? and, Do I have the means to migrate? Many factors will go into determining the answer to those questions. Some of these will be unique to the migrants themselves: their personal situation, their characteristics and those of their families, or the perceived risks and opportunities from staying or leaving. Yet others will be determined at a higher level: what the economic and safety situation is inside the village, province, or country where they live; how laws and institutions restrict or promote relocation; or how a changing natural resource base or climate affects lives and livelihoods.

These factors will also play a critical role in the *type* of migration a migrant undertakes. A dry season or other short-term event that reduces agricultural wages is more likely to lead to seasonal or short-term migration, whereas a catastrophic event, such as a deep or prolonged drought, devastating flood, or conflict, will be more likely to lead to increased numbers of permanent relocations. Similarly, the distribution of opportunities, international laws, and individual migrant characteristics will be factors that determine whether migrants relocate domestically or internationally.

Even though across the world three out of four migrants move within their countries' national borders, this form of migration tends to be underrecognized in global policy discussions. For this reason, *Ebb and Flow: Volume 1. Water, Migration, and Development* mainly considers domestic migrants. *Ebb and Flow: Volume 2. Water in the Shadow of Conflict in the Middle East and North Africa* (Borgomeo et al. 2021), however, focuses on a region that is particularly beset with water and forced displacement challenges. Given the larger number—both in relative and absolute terms—of forcibly displaced people in the region, and the unique concerns related to conflict, *Ebb and Flow: Volume 2,* has a broader focus than this volume does.

The water sector, and the availability of water itself, is implicit or explicit in many of these migration factors. While water is by no means the only or even the main driver of migration, it has the ability to amplify the existing movements of people and add urgency to the challenges faced by these migrants. Being a basic requirement for survival, a critical input into all forms of production, a force for destruction in areas lacking resilient infrastructure, and a resource that can lead to conflict or cooperation between and within countries, water has the power to shape migration and development patterns. Acting through these pathways, water availability, extreme events, infrastructure, and policies can have long-lasting impacts on growth and development. While much has been written and studied on these topics at the regional or local level, this report uses a global lens and attempts to shed light on three critical questions (figure ES.1):

FIGURE ES.1: This Report Takes a Global Perspective to Answer Three Questions

Sending region •---• Receiving region

1 WHY MIGRATE?	2 WHO MIGRATES?	3 WHERE AND WHAT IMPACTS?
Why and in what context do water shocks influence migration and development?	Who migrates because of water shocks and what does this mean for productivity and livelihoods?	What are the impacts of migration, where do they occur, and what are the broader implications for development?

Source: World Bank.

1. **Why and in what context do water shocks influence migration and development?** This report, for the first time, attempts to take a global view of the link between water, migration, and development. It finds that there are important nuances to the idea of a "water migrant" that have critical implications for designing policies to make communities more resilient.

2. **Who migrates because of water shocks and what does this mean for productivity and livelihoods?** To examine these factors, the report zooms in on the characteristics of migrants, including those who may migrate involuntarily.

3. **What are the impacts of migration, where do the impacts occur, and what are the broader implications for development?** Cities, which are often the destination of migrants, are believed to be more resilient to water shocks than rural locations. This report provides evidence against this conjecture, finding that water shocks can have significant impacts in urban areas.

To explore these questions, several novel national and global-level data sets have been combined for the first time. Such data include global precipitation data covering the extent of the 20th and 21st centuries, which allow the researchers to flexibly and locally determine when an area is experiencing a water deficit or excess; data sets that link cities to their water sources to identify when urban water supplies are likely to run lower; new spatially disaggregated data on local migration rates; household surveys and government censuses; and data on nighttime lights to track economic activity. By merging these data sets and employing multiple statistical techniques that rely on machine learning and causal inference, new insights are gained that may not have been apparent or may even run counter to intuition and expectations. In this way, the report examines impacts in rural areas, the primary focus of chapter 2; urban areas, the primary focus of chapter 4; and migrants in both types of regions, the focus of chapter 3.

Given the myriad ways the water sector can influence migration and development, there is a need to reduce the dimensionality of the question and focus on a few areas of critical importance. Water stress can occur for many different geoclimatic and anthropogenic reasons: weather anomalies such as those that accompany climate change; the presence of weak institutions around irrigation and water markets; and sudden population growth such as those brought about by forced displacement; among many others. To ensure that the scope of this report is limited to evidence-based discussions, arguments and recommendations are informed by statistical analyses that exploit unanticipated changes in the weather and isolate the impact of water availability.

This report focuses on changes in water availability that are induced by "rainfall shocks," a term used here to mean that rainfall is significantly above or below the long-run average for that region. Rainfall shocks can be of both the *wet* kind, in which a region sees significantly above-average rainfall, and the *dry* kind, in which a region sees significant rainfall deficits. Dry rainfall shocks can translate into water deficits when they lead to a reduction in available water supplies in lakes and reservoirs (as discussed more in chapter 4). Although significant attention is often paid to responses to catastrophic events, less attention is given to slower-moving cumulative effects of climate change, such as repeated dry or wet shocks. Because migration and development entail long-term consequences, the analyses in the report examine the effects of consecutive shocks and not just immediate impacts.

Taking a Global, Long-Run Perspective

Before turning to the why, who, and where of water and migration, a more fundamental question must be asked: How much of a role does water play in global migration? Although there is a growing body of research investigating the migration–environment relationship in a variety of settings, most studies cover select geographic areas or countries. While there is growing evidence that weather conditions are linked to migration rates in many regions, no study to date has compared the impact of rainfall shocks with other well-known determinants of migration to see just how important these shocks are in the grand scheme.

To shed light on the link between water shocks and migration, this report employed the largest data set on migration ever assembled. This includes data from over 442 million individuals from 189 different population censuses in 64 countries between 1960 and 2015. With such large amounts of data, standard econometric analysis becomes infeasible and new techniques for data analysis must be employed. Hence, a machine learning model—random forests—was employed. The analysis tests how strongly rainfall deficits, as measured by periods of low rainfall relative to long-run averages, are related to migration decisions, relative to other variables that are well established to be crucial for determining whether a person migrates: a person's age, gender, educational level, household size, and marital status. Although the results in this particular analysis do not represent causal relationships, they are useful for establishing if any relationship at all exists between water and migration, before the report digs deeper into causal analysis.

The results show that rainfall deficits are significant predictors of population movements within countries around the world. Figure ES.2 shows the results from the machine learning analysis. Each dot in the figure shows the importance of each characteristic for explaining migration in a given country relative to education, which is used as a benchmark because it is a critical determinant of migration. Not surprisingly, age and household size are more important than education and have the largest explanatory power for regional out-migration on average. Other characteristics, such as gender or marital status, are, on average, as relevant as education. Critically, the results also show that periods of low rainfall can wield a considerable influence on migration outcomes in addition to the traditional drivers of migration. Even though the occurrence of these dry rainfall shocks is slightly less important than education, the box plot in figure ES.2 shows that, in contrast to individual characteristics, the range of importance varies considerably, and in some countries dry rainfall shocks can be as important as gender, marital status, or even education.

FIGURE ES.2: The Importance of Various Characteristics in Explaining Migration

Random forest model explaining migration in 64 countries
Relative explanatory power of various characteristics (education = 100)

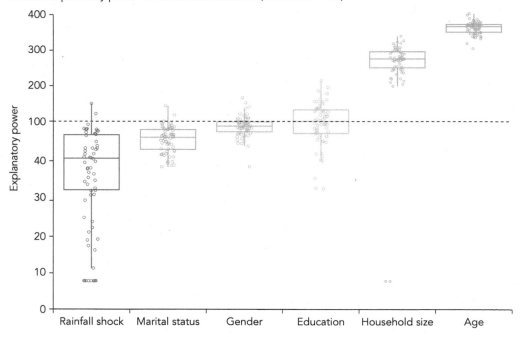

Source: World Bank figure based on data from 189 different censuses and weather data from Matsuura and Willmott 2018.

Note: The figure summarizes the results of 189 estimates derived using random forest techniques to explain the importance of various characteristics in explaining migration behavior. Each dot represents the results from a different country/year. The y-axis shows how critical each variable along the x-axis is for explaining migration in that country/year. Values are normalized with respect to education, such that the mean value of education takes a value of 100, and all other countries are shown relative to education's explanatory power, with values over (under) 100 implying that the value is more (less) important for explaining migration patterns.

Stay or Go: Why and in What Context Do Water Shocks Induce Migration?

Media reports and attention-grabbing articles are often awash with headlines warning of massive waves of "water refugees." While increasing water scarcity and climate change will undoubtedly lead to an increasing number of national and international migrants, there are important nuances to this story. Understanding these is critical to developing strategies to help households cope with water shocks, thus easing the migration transition or preventing the need entirely. To examine these nuances, the report draws on research that employs a granular data set of net migration rates covering more than 150 countries over a 30-year time period.

The results demonstrate that while water shocks are a significant driver of migration, there are surprising and critically important intervening factors in this relationship. Using statistical methods that allow for causal inference leads to the finding that water deficits result in five times as much migration as do water deluges, despite the fact that floods are much more likely to gain national or international attention. Overall, rainfall deficits explain approximately 10 percent of the increase in migration that has occurred around the world between 1970 and 2000.

The migration response to rainfall deficits varies significantly depending on country income, with the poorest 80 percent less likely to migrate in the face of these shocks. This is because migration is often a costly endeavor, with significant transaction costs needed to sell or transport assets, find a new place to live, and seek out a new means of supporting oneself and one's family. For the most vulnerable members of society, the migration option may therefore not be available. These trapped populations can find themselves facing a triple whammy: water deficits, reduced economic opportunities in their region, and no means to move to places with more opportunities. While they are often hidden from media headlines, they represent a policy concern just as serious as migration. As shown in figure ES.3, poorer households might need to experience beneficial wet episodes that allow them to raise the necessary funds to migrate.

Water, Migration, and Human Capital Spillovers: Who Are the Typical Migrants and What Human Capital Do They Carry with Them?

The movement of human capital is a key channel through which migration influences regional development. Migration within an economy allows for the sorting of workers within large cities and industrial regions to contribute to the sectors in which they have a comparative advantage. It also

FIGURE ES.3: Impact of Rainfall Shocks on Out-Migration Rates, by Income

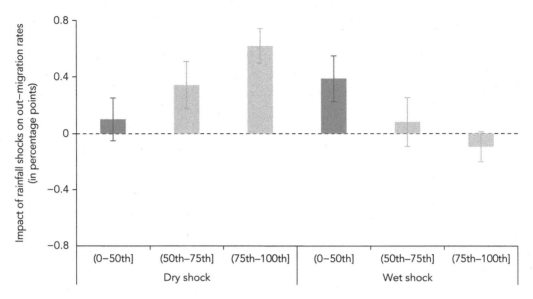

Source: World Bank figure based on analysis using global estimated net migration data by de Sherbinin et al. 2015, population data from Yamagata and Murakami 2015, and weather data from Matsuura and Willmott 2018. *Note:* Figure ES.3 shows point estimates of an additional dry or wet rainfall shock on the out-migration rate by the bottom and top two quartiles of the income per capita distribution with 95 percent confidence intervals. The vertical axis shows the impact on out-migration rates in percentage points.

acts as an insurance option available to poorer households for coping with a lack of on-farm economic opportunities. The different motivations and constraints that drive migration produce different types of migrants. The United States' experience of the Dust Bowl in the 1930s, for instance, led to the movement of the archetypal climate migrant: the poor displaced farmer responding to adverse climate conditions. Unexpected income losses for farmers due to drought conditions can force the migration of lower-skilled individuals who would not have moved otherwise.

This report analyzes regional data on migrants and their schooling in conjunction with climate data and shows that drier conditions are causally linked to more low-skilled migration than would occur otherwise. Workers who move from rural to urban areas in developing countries because of drier climate conditions are less likely to have high education levels (figure ES.4). These workers are typically less productive and can face upto a 3.4 percent wage gap in their host regions as compared to the typical migrant. Wetter conditions are not found to have any consistent effect.

In rapidly urbanizing middle-income countries, droughts are found to increase the flow of lower-skilled workers from rural to urban areas. In more arid regions, this effect of rainfall shortages on the type of migrant

FIGURE ES.4: **Rainfall and Migrants' Education**

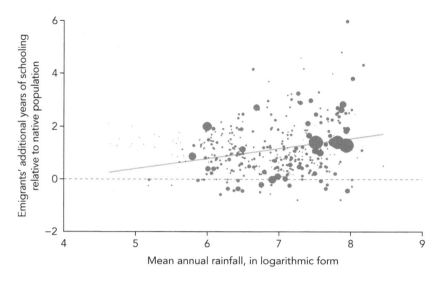

Source: World Bank figure based on analysis of demographic and economic data of 403 subnational regions covering 21 developing countries from Gennaioli et al. 2013 and climate data from Matsuura and Willmott 2018. *Note:* The figure shows that (internal) migrants originating from regions with higher average rainfall levels have higher years of schooling relative to natives in the place of origin. The size of the bubble is proportional to the population of the subnational region.

is mitigated, likely because agriculture and irrigation have adapted over time to these shortages. The presence of local employment opportunities for unemployed farm workers in rural areas is also found to be critical for mitigating low-skilled migration as a reaction to drier conditions. In sum, differences in economic structure, climate characteristics, and regional specificities caution against sweeping conclusions.

The Cost of Day Zero Events: What Are the Development Implications for Shocks in the City?

While much of what is written on the water–migration–development nexus focuses on how water shocks push people from rural areas into cities, very little is written on what happens when cities experience these shocks. Unprecedented urbanization rates, driven partially by the factors previously discussed, are causing some cities to expand faster than water and other critical services can sustain. These growing populations, coupled with a surge in per capita demand for water in cities, are expected to translate to an 80 percent increase in demand for water in urban areas by 2050. And climate change is altering the global hydrologic cycle, increasing the number of extreme episodes and making water supplies less predictable. Recent headlines from Chennai, Tamil Nadu, India; São Paulo, Brazil; and

Cape Town, South Africa show some of the world's megacities are beginning to face day zero events whereby water supplies become threateningly low. Although these events have grabbed international attention, they are by no means unique, with scores of small cities throughout both the developed and developing world facing similar water shortages.

New research conducted for this report on the impact of day zero events finds that they are far more widespread than previously believed and that they have significant economic costs, slowing down urban growth. Water shortages, and the resulting restrictions that are put in place to avoid day zero events, can be costly to people and to businesses. In Cape Town, ill-equipped households were forced to ration water to 50 liters per day. In São Paulo, water pressure in the city's piped network was reduced, restricting water flow to businesses and households alike. Undoubtedly these types of restrictions translate into economic impacts, though the magnitude of these impacts has, until now, remained unexplored.

This report finds that such water shortages can significantly slow urban growth, compounding the vulnerability of migrants. Depending on the size of the water shock, city growth can slow by up to 12 percent during drought years, enough to reverse critical development progress (figure ES.5). Thus, migrants who travel to cities to avoid the impacts of

---

FIGURE ES.5: Impact of Rainfall Shocks on City Growth Rates at Urban Water Points

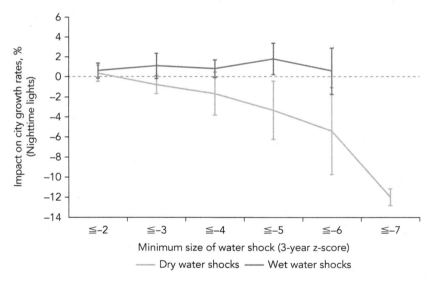

Source: World Bank figure based on analysis using weather data from Matsuura and Willmott 2018; Nighttime Lights Time Series Version 4, from NOAA National Centers for Environmental Information, Earth Observation Group; and data on urban water sources from The Nature Conservancy and McDonald 2016.
Note: Figure shows point estimates of the impact of increasingly large water shocks on urban economic activity with 95 percent confidence intervals.

rainfall variability may find themselves in cities that offer fewer economic opportunities and critical services than expected. Evidence from the report finds that cities in more arid areas may be better equipped to handle these water shortages and do not face as much of an impact on growth as areas in more humid regions. Similar heterogeneities also exist between small and large cities, with larger cities being more resilient against water shocks.

Going with the Flow: The Policy Challenge

The results presented in this report demonstrate that the popular image of droughts or floods driving waves of destitute migrants is a misleading caricature. While water shocks certainly amplify existing movements and migrations, the idea of a "water migrant" as a singular concept is an unhelpful and overly broad generalization. Indeed, the report finds that it is the poorest individuals who often lack the means to migrate, even when doing so might improve their livelihoods and prospects. They remain stuck in areas blighted by drought with few opportunities for advancement. Those people who are able to migrate often arrive in cities that are ill prepared to receive them, supply them with basic services, or take advantage of their skills. And many of these cities, far from being bastions of resilience themselves, are increasingly suffering from water shortages and economic slowdowns.

    There is no single silver bullet solution to addressing climate-induced migration, and an arsenal of overlapping and complementary policies will be needed to improve livelihoods and turn crises into opportunities for growth. The way in which governments respond will either implicitly or explicitly influence decisions to migrate, thereby changing the destinies of people and the development trajectories of regions. Policies that focus on eliminating risks at the source may tacitly discourage migration by promoting rural livelihoods and thus slowing urban demographic growth. On the other hand, policies that promote the integration of migrants at their destinations would make migration more attractive, thus accelerating movement and promoting growth in cities. The appropriate policy response will likely vary over time and across locations.

    In situ policies that aim at reducing risks at the source can be classified into three broad categories: physical infrastructure, natural capital, and safety nets.

- **Water storage and supplemental irrigation can be effective at buffering vulnerable rural communities against water variability and scarcity and lessening the impact of rainfall deficits on migration, but there are caveats.** Providing irrigation water supplies at little or no charge sends a signal that water is abundant, even when it is scarce. This often results in water-intensive cropping systems that deplete water resources faster than they can be replenished. The result is often a less resilient agricultural system and higher vulnerability than existed before the provision of irrigation services. Thus, while these investments are necessary, they must be combined with regulations and policies that promote more judicious use.

- **In addition, investments in physical infrastructure can generate perverse incentives and "moral hazard" problems, whereby the presence of infrastructure incentivizes people to remain in, or even move to, regions that are hydrologically and ecologically unable to support growing populations in the long run.** In regions such as these, where sluggish migration traps people in nonviable places, the focus should be on removing barriers to mobility rather than on place-based policies. Poor countries face a host of market frictions that can deter mobility. In addition to restricted budgets that make it costly to migrate in response to droughts, implicit barriers from residency-based access to public services and safety nets as well as informational asymmetry and distortions in land and housing markets can also deter mobility. Investing in mobility can be an investment in the future by reducing vulnerabilities and increasing incentives for autonomous risk reduction, which discourages building in areas that are clearly exposed to high climate risks.

- **New evidence presented in this report suggests another reason to be cautious when deciding where to invest in irrigation systems.** Large-scale irrigation investments in resource-scarce settings are often at risk of becoming magnets for conflict. For instance, after the disruptions caused during the Arab Spring, irrigated regions of North Africa and the G5 Sahel (Burkina Faso, Chad, Mali, Mauritania, and Niger) countries experienced higher incidences of conflict in irrigated areas. This finding suggests that decisions that alter access to shared resources may need to be accompanied by complementary investments in governance, institutions, and effective social protection systems for the poorest and most vulnerable populations.

- **Improved hydrometeorological forecasting is another important means of mitigating the consequences of weather fluctuations for populations at the source.** Accurate and timely climate, weather, and water resources information is an example of a technology-intensive public good that has minimal delivery costs and can substantially reduce the principal source of income risk for the poor. The returns to enhancing individual risk reduction by improving the accuracy of annual and interannual weather forecasts are potentially high, given the small costs of delivery.

- **Climate smart agriculture (CSA) and farmer-led irrigation can also buffer rural livelihoods from climate change and increasing rainfall variability while minimizing the environmental footprint.**

Through a combination of smart policies, financing, and technologies, CSA can achieve a triple win by increasing productivity, enhancing resilience, and reducing greenhouse gas emissions. And farmer-led irrigation can ensure that small- and large-holder farmers alike can reap the benefits of irrigation investments, building resilience against climate and economic shocks in a more inclusive and sustainable way.

- **Either in conjunction with, or in lieu of, physical infrastructure, green infrastructure is usually more cost-effective at providing protection against droughts and floods.** Watersheds and their associated forests store, filter, and gradually distribute both surface water and groundwater, and as a result enhance the resilience and quality of water supplies. Forests are also a vital source of drought-proof income for the rural poor, who often obtain a greater share of their incomes from forest resources than from agriculture. Forests can therefore act as a "green safety net" in times of drought.

- **This report finds evidence that in areas where forest cover is high, out-migration in response to droughts is low or negligible.** Nature-based solutions can also be significantly more cost-effective than built infrastructure. On average it would cost about US$0.8 trillion to US$3 trillion in irrigation infrastructure to compensate for the buffering effects of lost natural capital due to a 10 percentage point decrease in the share of forested land. Investing in complementary solutions to buffer incomes—for example, protecting watersheds and forests, together with a canal or dam for irrigation—produces greater benefits than investing in any single one of these solutions.

- **Safety net programs, such as cash and in-kind transfers, are critical as a last backstop to prevent severe deprivation when water shocks hit.** Even moderate deprivation at sensitive times in a person's development can lead to lifelong challenges such as stunting, chronic health problems, and loss of educational opportunities. In some cases, these impacts can be transmitted through generations, perpetuating the cycle of poverty. While the provision of irrigation infrastructure and natural capital solutions may provide buffers that reduce the impacts of drought, inevitably some residual risks will remain.

Ex situ policy options that aim to improve the situation at destinations—which are often urban areas—must be considered in tandem with in situ policy options at the source. These include providing better integration of rural migrants into urban settings and making cities more resilient to water shocks.

- **The net economic effect of migrants at the destination will depend on how well they are socially and economically integrated into their**

new homes. While this report does find evidence that drought migrants tend to be less educated than the average migrant who moves to a host city, a conclusion that these migrants are drains on urban economies would be unfounded. Migrants also bring beneficial economic effects, such as stimulating demand for housing and other nontradable goods and services within a city and bringing complementary skills that could yield net economic benefits, as is seen in migrant enclaves of many cities around the world. The overall economic effect is a priori ambiguous and will be determined by local conditions and the capacity of the destination to absorb a larger labor force of lower-skilled workers.

- **The precise policy mix will vary across countries, but there are several fundamental ingredients for migrant integration that should be followed across most contexts.** Poor migrants who live in informal settlements often endure high levels of violence and insecurity and lack basic services such as water supply and sanitation, schools, and health care, and they reside in unsafe housing. Efforts made to improve these services will pay large dividends, both to the migrants themselves and to the broader city. In the COVID-19 context, particular attention is warranted to health and water supply and sanitation systems, which are critical in slowing the spread of diseases. Active labor market policies that build skills through various support and training modalities (such as "schools beyond walls") and integrate migrants into labor markets are also important for ensuring migrants can take advantage of the economic opportunities that cities have to offer. "No regrets" solutions, such as investments in workers' education and training, will be critical to ensure that workers can be productive wherever they may choose to locate.

- **As the challenge to absorb the growing demands of urban populations and shocks to water supplies increase, city planners will increasingly need to build resilient cities.** As highlighted previously, cities are growing at breakneck speed and critical public services, such as water management and water supply provision, often struggle to keep up. And as the 21st century progresses, the more climate change is expected to exacerbate these underlying vulnerabilities.

- **There is no simple solution to addressing water shortages in cities, but smart policies can reduce their propensity for damage and their impacts.** Increasing water supply through desalination or other supply-augmenting technologies may seem like a quick fix, though history shows that these endeavors can be risky and inefficient. This was learned by the city of Sydney, which, after facing a severe and extended water shortage, invested in a large and costly desalination plant only to find that by the time the plant was operational the drought had ended and the plant was no longer needed.

- **Demand-side management might offer a way forward that is less costly and less risky.** Dynamically efficient volumetric water pricing, for instance, can adjust the price of water to better match the scarcity that cities are facing. By allowing utilities to carefully adjust the price of water on the basis of its scarcity, utilities can avoid the need to invest in water-augmenting technologies and thus save money, reduce water footprints, and keep water costs lower in the long run. Other technologies, such as smart water meters and water-saving and reusing appliances, offer ways to help households reduce their water footprint with little sacrifice.

- **Water reallocation may offer another solution for ever-thirstier cities.** Flexible approaches that allow for emergency transfers of water when needed can insure cities against extreme droughts. Drought option contracts could give the city the right to buy a set quantity of water at agreed prices in the event of a drought. Since the option would only be exercised under agreed weather conditions, this would also preserve the water for agriculture during normal situations.

- **Better urban planning is also sorely needed.** Cities, and the impervious concrete foundations on which they lie, block drainage patterns and cause water to run though the city—causing floods—and then away from the city, creating a missed opportunity. Instead, cities should be redesigned to resemble sponges to soak up that water, store it below ground for future use, and prevent it from damaging the above-ground structures. Doing so involves using permeable material in paving, building storage ponds, preserving key wetlands, and building more green spaces, including rooftop gardens. Actions like these will improve urban water security and ensure that the bright lights of cities remain attractive to future migrants and current residents alike.

Much uncertainty exists around the future, and for policy makers and migrants alike, it will be difficult to predict the eventual outcome of the decision to migrate. Nevertheless, in the words of Nobel Prize winner Amartya Sen (1999), "Development consists of the removal of various types of unfreedoms that leave people with little choice and little opportunity of exercising their reasoned agency. The removal of substantial unfreedoms…is constitutive of development." By removing restrictions on internal migration, even if not directly incentivizing it, governments help individuals gain agency to determine the outcome that is best for themselves. At a minimum, lifting political restrictions within countries and easing the integration of migrants into communities can reduce the number of people unnecessarily trapped in regions that are becoming less and less life sustaining.

With limited resources, governments need to choose policies that are most effective in dealing with the adverse consequences of

rainfall-induced migration, especially in the fiscally constrained post-COVID-19 context. This report suggests the need for synchronized and complementary policies, recognizing that no single policy can adequately address the many impacts of a rainfall shock. For instance, infrastructure, while essential, will not be fully effective in eliminating all risks to incomes and well-being. Addressing these residual risks to incomes might call for safety nets, especially for the most vulnerable. And while a safety net may provide minimum resources necessary for survival, it would not provide the protection to assets and businesses that may be required to spur investment in the affected areas. In such circumstances, infrastructure and safety nets combined would be more effective in drought-proofing communities. Ultimately, policies that focus on reducing the impacts of water shocks must be complemented by strategies that broaden opportunities and build the long-term resilience of communities.

On the following pages, figures ES.6 and ES.7 summarize the main results and policy recommendations of *Ebb and Flow: Volume 1*.

FIGURE ES.6: Water Shapes Migration and Development

WATER SHAPES MIGRATION AND DEVELOPMENT

Water deficits explain **10%** of the rise in total migration

Water deficits result in **5** times as much migration as water excess

Why

Migration can act as a **release valve** when droughts induce income shocks

But **not everyone** has the option to move:

Droughts can trap the poorest households

Low-income country residents are 80% less likely to be able to move than higher-income residents

Who

Droughts can also influence **who** migrates

Workers moving out of regions with lower rainfall bring with them **lower skills** which affects **economic productivity** in receiving regions

Migrants escaping droughts face a wage gap of up to 3.4% when they arrive at their destination

Where

Cities are the destination of most migrants who are **escaping droughts**

But even in cities **droughts** can **haunt migrants**

Day zero-like events, where cities almost **run out of water** are more frequent than we realize

These events can reduce urban growth by up to 12 percentage points

Source: World Bank.

FIGURE ES.7: Policies and Investments to Sustain Prosperity

POLICIES AND INVESTMENTS TO SUSTAIN PROSPERITY

Policies to manage water risks need to **target people and places**

Complementary policies are needed to turn water crises into opportunities

Protect livelihoods in the place of origin

Climate smart agriculture
Build resilience to longer term stresses and reduce vulnerability to climate shocks

A balanced portfolio of Gray and Green infrastructure
Water storage and supplemental irrigation buffer income from water shocks and influence incentives to migrate

Forests provide drought-proof income for the rural poor and healthy ecosystems provide cost-effective risk mitigation

Hydromet service
Building monitoring capacity for timely and accurate information

People-centered investments

Human capital investments
Education is a portable asset that moves with people wherever they go

Safety nets
Adaptive safety nets and transfers provide insurance from severe water shocks

Integration of migrants
Integrative labor market policies enable migrants to find the best opportunities, and basic service delivery bolsters productivity

Preserve and sustain resources in cities

Urban planning
Smarter cities that capture and reuse water can build resilience to floods and droughts

Demand-side management of water
Water pricing with targeted subsidies are needed to reduce demand when supplies are constrained

Adaptive Water Reallocation
Emergency option contracts that trigger reallocation at agreed prices can insure against severe drought

Source: World Bank.

References

Borgomeo, Edoardo, Anders Jägerskog, Esha Zaveri, Jason Russ, Amjad Khan, and Richard Damania. 2021. *Ebb and Flow: Volume 2. Water in the Shadow of Conflict in the Middle East and North Africa.* Washington, DC: World Bank.

Clement, V., K. K. Rigaud, A. de Sherbinin, B. Jones, S. Adamo, J. Schewe, N. Sadiq, and E. Shabahat. 2021. "Groundswell Part II: Acting on Internal Climate Migration." World Bank, Washington, DC.

de Sherbinin, A., M. Levy, S. Adamo, K. MacManus, G. Yetman, V. Mara, L. Razafindrazay, B. Goodrich, T. Srebotnjak, C. Aichele, and L. Pistolesi. 2015. "Global Estimated Net Migration Grids by Decade: 1970–2000." NASA Socioeconomic Data and Applications Center (SEDAC), Palisades, NY.

Gennaioli, N., R. La Porta, F. Lopez-de-Silanes, and A. Shleifer. 2013. "Human Capital and Regional Development." *Quarterly Journal of Economics* 128 (1): 105–64.

Lall, S. V., M. S. M. Lebrand, H. Park, D. M. Sturm, and A. J. Venables. 2021. *Pancakes to Pyramids: City Form to Promote Sustainable Growth.* Washington, DC: World Bank Group.

Matsuura, K., and C. J. Willmott. 2018. *Terrestrial Air Temperature and Precipitation: Monthly and Annual Time Series (1900–2017).* http://climate .geog.udel.edu/~climate/html_pages/download.html.

The Nature Conservancy and R. McDonald. 2016. "City Water Map (version 2.2). KNB Data Repository. doi:10.5063/F1J67DWR." Accessed through Resource Watch. www.resourcewatch.org.

Sen, A. 1999. *Development as Freedom.* Oxford: Oxford University Press.

Yamagata, Y., and D. Murakami. 2015. "Global Dataset of Gridded Population and GDP Scenarios." Center for Global Environmental Research, Tsukuba International Office, Global Carbon Project, Tsukuba, Japan.

CHAPTER ONE

TRANSITIONS AND TRANSFORMATIONS

"An ideal society should be mobile, should be full of channels for conveying a change taking place in one part to other parts."

– Bhimrao Ramji Ambedkar, chief drafter of India's Constitution

INTRODUCTION

Understanding the fundamental role of movement in the process of economic development has long intrigued scholars, philosophers, and policy makers. Six centuries ago, and some 400 years before Adam Smith wrote the classic treatise *An Inquiry into the Nature and Causes of the Wealth of Nations*, the Arab scholar Ibn Khaldun proposed a theory of cyclical development whereby the parallel movements of population, urbanization, and public finance determined the rise and fall of civilizations (Weiss 1995).

He was clearly onto something. Without the movement of goods, people, and ideas, economies can wane and stagnate. Movement can fuel growth and propel the dispersion and agglomeration of interlinked activities. It can even out standards of living across regions and help absorb economic shocks. Not surprisingly, all development experiences and growth episodes in history have involved a reallocation of factors of production, such as labor and capital, across space and sectors within countries (World Bank 2018). It is for this reason that the simple observation that rich countries are industrial and poor countries are agricultural has prompted many development thinkers since Ibn Khaldun to conclude that countries develop when they shift factors of production, especially labor, from an unproductive "traditional" sector—such as subsistence farming—to "modern" sectors such as manufacturing and services. The internal migration of workers to urban areas, in particular, is a recurring theme in modern theories of development. Even today, a great majority of people migrate internally, with almost three times as many people migrating within countries than internationally (McAuliffe and Ruhs 2017). Resources such as water often play a critical role in the decision to move (box 1.1).

From the earliest days, rains, rivers, coasts, and seas have shaped the spatial distribution of economic activity (Amrith 2018) (box 1.2). Tales from classical antiquity to the Abrahamic religions to ancient Mesopotamia speak of how water has reshaped societies. More fundamentally, water has the potential to influence the process of economic transformation by impacting movement and migration. The availability of water can have a large effect on where people choose to live and work and the skills they carry. In turn, the regions where people settle require access to adequate water resources—accompanied by commensurate infrastructure investments— to sustain growth and allow populations to survive and thrive. *Ebb and Flow: Volume 1* presents new evidence on some of these foundational development issues to examine the nexus where water, migration decisions, and economic development converge.

FOCUS OF THE REPORT

The focus of this report is not meant to be exhaustive in relation to the water and migration nexus. The issues related to the impacts of water on mobility are wide ranging, with endless ramifications and enormous knowledge gaps. Addressing all of these challenges is beyond the scope of the report. Instead, the primary, though not exclusive, focus of the report is to examine the role of fluctuations in water availability, or "water shocks," in influencing three critical questions (figure 1.1):

1. **Why and in what context do water shocks influence migration and development?** This report, for the first time, attempts to take a global view of the link between water, migration, and development. It finds that there are important nuances to the idea of a "water migrant" that have critical implications for designing policies to make communities more resilient.

2. **Who migrates because of water shocks and what does this mean for productivity and livelihoods?** To examine these factors, the report zooms in on the characteristics of internal migrants, including those who may migrate involuntarily.

BOX 1.1: Water and the Urbanizing Force of Development

The observed shift of populations "out of agriculture," often noted as "structural transformation," was a central focus of influential early scholarship by many economic historians and development thinkers (see Rosenstein-Rodan 1943; Lewis 1954; Rostow 1960; and Harris and Todaro 1970). These issues even captured the attention of classical economists decades earlier, as exemplified by the famous Soviet debates of the 1920s that centered around whether to "squeeze" farmer surpluses to hasten industrialization (Preobrazhensky 1921). In aggregate, scholars agree that reallocation of factors of production, which includes rural–urban mobility, remains an important channel through which structural transformation occurs. Internal migration leads to urbanization, which, in turn, induces economic growth (Lagakos 2020). In China, for instance, the easing of mobility constraints and migration costs at the turn of the twenty-first century allowed for increased internal migration. The resulting move of workers out of rural areas and into cities is estimated to have increased aggregate labor productivity by 5 percent and welfare by 11 percent (Tombe and Zhu 2019).

Can changes generated by water shocks eventually lead to a long-term structural transformation of the economy and improve welfare? Or will they slow down the process? The answer is not straightforward and depends on the complex interplay between the social, economic, and natural environments. Water availability and variability induced by climate, geography, policies, and infrastructure can constrain or incentivize the movement of workers. Increased mobility can bring large economic benefits, while constraints on internal migration can lead to a misallocation of (labor) resources, exacerbate inequality, and generate large losses in total productivity within and across countries (Hsieh and Klenow 2010; Restuccia and Rogerson 2017).

In the early stages of development, for instance, water availability can boost agricultural productivity and generate the economic surpluses necessary to release or "pull" labor into the nonagricultural sector (Gollin, Parente, and Rogerson 2002; Michaels, Rauch, and Redding 2012; Emerick 2018). Because adverse water conditions make agriculture less productive, they could also potentially "push" labor out of agriculture and into other sectors, while also, in many instances, drive migration as a consequence (Fishman, Jain, and Kishore 2017; Henderson, Storeygard, and Deichmann 2017; Chen and Mueller 2018; Colmer 2018; Blakeslee, Fishman, and Srinivasan 2020). Investigating the underlying migration mechanisms and their interactions with water can shed light on some of these foundational development issues.

3. **What are the impacts of migration, where do they occur, and what are the broader implications for development?** Cities, which are often the destination of migrants, are believed to be more resilient to water shocks than rural locations are. This report provides evidence against this conjecture, finding that water shocks can have significant impacts in urban areas.

In this way, the report sheds light on how fluctuations in the availability of water determine mobility, the flow of human capital, and the process of economic development itself. Although much has been written and studied on these topics at the regional or local level, this report takes a step back and provides a global view of the issues with new findings.

These questions are all the more salient as climate change worsens stresses on the water cycle. The increasing variability and uncertainty of rainfall can weigh heavily on communities and economies. Rainfall shocks—anomalies whereby precipitation is well below or above normal levels—are already becoming more frequent, and coping with them may present one of the most difficult challenges confronting humanity. Indeed, a large body of recent work at the development policy and humanitarian nexus has recognized and

BOX 1.2: Is Water a Locational Fundamental?

Access to a reliable water source has historically been a fundamental necessity to sustain human settlements at any given location. Archaeological evidence suggests that populations migrated where there was adequate water availability; as a result, the geographic distribution of water remains one of the locational fundamentals that have shaped the spatial distribution of economic activity over the course of history (Gupta et al. 2006). Along some coasts, access to the rich bounty of the sea supported early coastal settlements, particularly in the lush delta regions of major rivers. Over time, these regions attracted more people, buoying economic growth and creating long-lasting civilizations that persist even today (Dalgaard, Knudsen, and Selaya 2020).

People have always located where there is access to water. Map B1.2.1 confirms this observation by plotting the locations of the largest cities and major rivers, with the size of the dots representing city size classes. The clustering of cities observed along major river basins reflects the integral role of water availability in determining where populations choose to settle. For instance, note the concentration of cities along the Ganges and Indus rivers, and in Sub-Saharan Africa. In contrast, note also the absence of cities in arid regions such as the Sahara and western China. In the same vein, the presence of water-yielding aquifers is also an important determinant of where housing is built and populations settle (Burchfield et al. 2006).

box continues next page

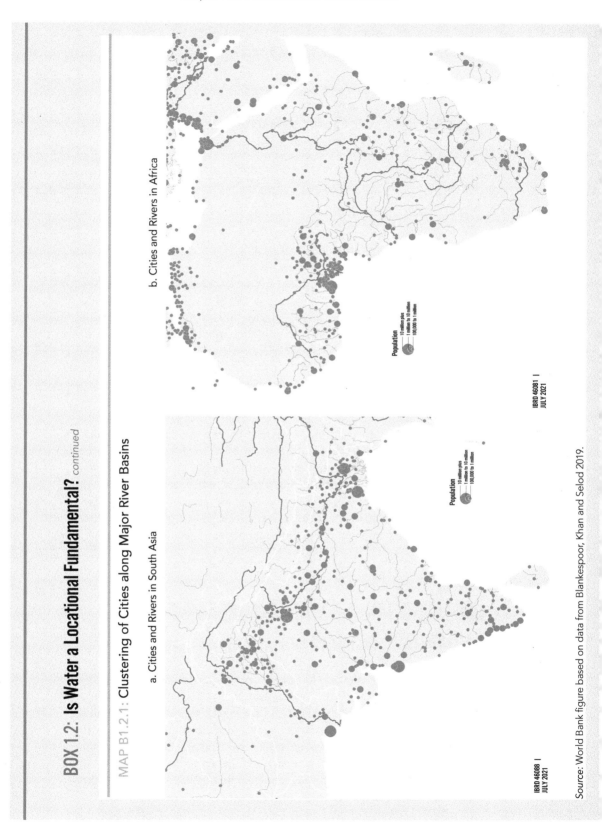

BOX 1.2: **Is Water a Locational Fundamental?** *continued*

MAP B1.2.1: Clustering of Cities along Major River Basins

a. Cities and Rivers in South Asia

b. Cities and Rivers in Africa

Population
10 million plus
1 million to 10 million
100,000 to 1 million

IBRD 46088 |
JULY 2021

IBRD 46081 |
JULY 2021

Source: World Bank figure based on data from Blankespoor, Khan and Selod 2019.

FIGURE 1.1: The Report Takes a Global Perspective to Address Three Questions

Sending region ●--● Receiving region

1

WHY MIGRATE?

Why and in what context do water shocks influence migration and development?

2

WHO MIGRATES?

Who migrates because of water shocks and what does this mean for productivity and livelihoods?

3

WHERE AND WHAT IMPACTS?

What are the impacts of migration, where do they occur, and what are the broader implications for development?

increasingly stressed the links between climate, water scarcity, and migration (Jägerskog and Swain 2016; Wrathall et al. 2018). Estimates by the World Bank suggest that in the absence of concrete action to reduce greenhouse gas emissions, more than 140 million migrants could be forced to move by 2050 due to climate change in Sub-Saharan Africa, South Asia, and Latin America alone (Rigaud et al. 2018).

Tragically, in the Middle East and North Africa, which is the most water-scarce region in the world and is home to 7.2 million refugees and 10.5 million internally displaced people, the interplay between water and migration is being enacted in the shadow of conflict. *Ebb and Flow: Volume 2* (Borgomeo et al. 2021), therefore, focuses on the complexities of the water–migration–conflict nexus in the Middle East and North Africa to examine how high levels of water stress interact with the movement of people, and the implications for resource-driven conflict. The COVID-19 pandemic has brought these challenges into even sharper relief through its impacts on the affordability and availability of water (box 1.3).

CLIMATE CHANGE AND THE INCREASING VARIABILITY OF RAINFALL

Water scarcity, stress, and climate change are typically portrayed through a lens of averages and trends. But this is seldom an adequate representation of water availability throughout much of the world, where deviations from trends and long-run averages are widespread and are growing more frequent. Adapting to rainfall variability is often much more challenging than accommodating long-term trends because of the unpredictable duration of a deviation, its uncertain magnitude, and its unknown frequency (Adams et al. 2013; World Bank 2021).

BOX 1.3: COVID-19 (Coronovirus) Fallout

The COVID-19 pandemic has caused a public health crisis unmatched in modern times. Along with the health crisis, the economic fallout has also been immense. Economies worldwide are expected to find themselves in moderate to deep recessions, with global economic output expected to be 5 percent below prepandemic projections (World Bank 2021). Large job losses and a significant impact on livelihoods are predicted, with dire consequences for poverty reduction, particularly in developing countries. Conservative estimates suggest that the resulting economic contraction will push about 150 million people into poverty worldwide (World Bank 2021).

The money that migrants send to their home regions is of special concern. Remittances have played an increasingly important role in alleviating poverty and sustaining growth. They also allow households in the home region to hedge against temporary shocks induced by weather variability or demand fluctuations. However, the COVID-19 crisis has spurred a dramatic reversal and resulted in an elimination of this insurance mechanism, leaving source areas at even greater risk of poverty, food insecurity, and income fluctuations. By the end of 2021, remittance flows to low- and middle-income countries are projected to fall by about 14 percent compared with pre-COVID-19 record levels of 2019 (Ratha et al. 2020). This loss is driven by both lower rates of migration due to existing migrants being sent home and new migrants unable to depart, as well as decreased remittances from those who remain away (Barker et al. 2020).

It is unclear how long the health effects of the pandemic will last; it will depend on the availability of effective vaccines at a global scale never before deployed. The spotlight at the end of this chapter, "Inequality, Social Cohesion, and the COVID-19 Public Health Crisis at the Nexus of Water and Migration", draws attention to the history of pandemics and highlights the importance of water-related investments in combating the disease as well as important policy lessons regarding the interplay between poverty, inequality, and social cohesion during such crises.

Impacts on the Forcibly Displaced in the Middle East and North Africa

In the Middle East and North Africa region, the pandemic has had profound implications for the forcibly displaced. Syrian refugees are a case in point, with at least 1.1 million in Lebanon, northern Jordan, and the Kurdistan region of Iraq driven into poverty as a result of the pandemic and related restrictions (Joint Data Center on Forced Displacement, World Bank Group, and UNHCR 2020).

Beyond the social and economic impacts, COVID-19 has also highlighted the challenges stemming from preexisting inequalities, such as differences in access to drinking water and water for hygiene, especially among excluded groups such as

box continues next page

BOX 1.3: COVID-19 (Coronovirus) Fallout *continued*

migrant populations. Residents of informal settlements that are characterized by crowding and shared water sources and sanitation facilities find themselves in hot spots for contagion and vulnerability (Bhardwaj et al. 2020), while for the forcibly displaced living in camps, access to the levels of water supply and sanitary items that support good hand hygiene is a daily challenge. In the words of Aziza, a Syrian refugee living in Amman who was interviewed as part of this study: "COVID-19 has greatly affected my daily life. My family's expenditure on detergents, soaps, and sanitizers has doubled." For others, COVID-19 has meant higher reliance and expenditure on water from tankers. As the world attempts to combat COVID-19 and prepare for future pandemics, *Ebb and Flow: Volume 2. Water in the Shadow of Conflict in the Middle East and North Africa* (Borgomeo et al. 2021) highlights priorities for maximizing the role of water, hygiene, and sanitation interventions in addressing pandemics in the Middle East and North Africa region.

In this volume, the role of water is examined via rainfall shocks (see box 1.4). For analytical purposes, these shocks are measured and characterized in terms of a statistical (that is, a "standard") deviation of rainfall from its long-term mean. Definitions of floods and droughts vary and often they are context specific, so the deviations analyzed in this report may not always be classified as either a drought or a flood. As an example, moderately wet episodes can boost agricultural productivity and economic growth but an unusually intense downpour may have catastrophic impacts. In addition, the report examines the impact of consecutive shocks. While more attention is paid to responses to catastrophic events, less attention is given to slower-moving effects of climate change such as repeated dry or wet shocks. Because migration and development entail long-term consequences, accounting for the temporal dimension of shocks is equally important.

Addressing the worsening problem of rainfall variability is not a distant challenge for the future. Over the past three decades, 1.8 billion people, or approximately 25 percent of humanity, have endured abnormal rainfall episodes each year, whether it was a particularly wet year or an unusually dry one (Damania et al. 2017). Unfortunately, variability has disproportionately impacted developing nations, with upward of 85 percent of affected people living in low- or middle-income countries (Damania et al. 2017). Many of the world's poorest countries, which have a disproportionately high dependence on agricultural employment, rapidly expanding populations, and elevated levels of water stress, endure strong variability of rainfall (Hall et al. 2014). Some scholars suggest that since the middle of the 20th century, anthropogenic climate forcing has doubled the joint probability of years that

BOX 1.4: Exploring Water Scarcity through Water Shocks

Water scarcity arises when the supply of water available in a region is unable to meet the local demand. People and places adapt over time to ensure that adequate water is provided to meet expected local consumption requirements. Local infrastructure and institutions coevolve with the concentration of economic activity and population in a region by responding to the demand-supply gap and the inflow of workers and capital into a region. This makes the issue of water scarcity difficult to quantify.

Water stress can occur for many different geoclimatic and anthropogenic reasons including weather anomalies such as those that will accompany climate change; the presence of weak institutions around irrigation and water markets; and sudden population growth such as those brought about by forced displacement. To reduce the dimensionality of the question, this report focuses on the effect of fluctuations in rainfall away from its long-term local average.

This approach of using "water shocks" induced by rainfall allows for analytic techniques that can isolate the impacts of water availability. Because they are unanticipated, these shocks act as natural experiments that allow for the comparison of economic outcomes in regions that experience them with regions that do not (or the same region but in a different year), much like a clinical trial would compare a treated population with a placebo group. By controlling for other critical characteristics that can influence the relationship, one can then isolate the impact that these shocks have on migration and development. Relying on such "water shocks" helps to provide a rigorous quantitative analysis of the impacts as well as an evidence-based discussion of policy implications for a range of related water-scarcity issues.

are both warm and dry in the same location, with the tropics and subtropics facing more record-breaking dry events (Lehmann, Mempel, and Coumou 2018; Sarhadi et al. 2018).

These effects are likely to intensify in the future with increases in both interannual and intraseasonal variability in some regions (World Bank, forthcoming). Often referred to as misery in slow motion, droughts are likely to become even more frequent and intense (Damania et al. 2017). Scientists warn that two thirds of the Earth's land is already on track to lose water, and by the late twenty-first century the global land area and population facing extreme droughts could more than double from 3 percent during 1976–2005 to 7–8 percent. These estimates mean that nearly 700 million people, or 8 percent of the projected future population, could be affected by extreme drought compared with 200 million over recent decades (Pokhrel et al. 2021).

LEARNING ABOUT WATER'S ROLE IN GLOBAL MIGRATION FROM HALF A BILLION INDIVIDUAL RECORDS

A vast body of research on the determinants and impacts of migration exists, reflecting its significance and sensitivity. More recently, an equally vast body of scholarship has investigated the migration–environment relationship in a variety of settings (see reviews by Millock 2015; Wrathall et al. 2018; Hoffman et al. 2020). These studies demonstrate considerable diversity in findings and reveal the contextually specific nature of the migration–environment relationship. But because most studies have been carried out in a localized context, it is often difficult to generalize the findings beyond the particular country or region analyzed.

To better understand water's role, this section explores a new avenue to test the predictive power of water indicators (along with other potential factors) for migration outcomes: machine learning. Machine learning algorithms are a powerful tool for detecting patterns that a human investigator may not discover. Although most machine learning models are unable to distinguish between mere correlations and causal relationships, they provide an indication of the factors that predict migration in a particular region, and the role that water plays in this decision (box 1.5).

BOX 1.5: Harnessing the Power of Machine Learning

Data. The assessment in this study is based on migration and sociodemographic data derived from harmonized census microdata samples from the Integrated Public Use Microdata Series, International database (Minnesota Population Center 2019). It provides the world's largest archive of publicly available census samples, with variables harmonized across countries and over time to facilitate comparative research. Samples are typically close to 10 percent of the entire census conducted by the national statistical agency in each country. The countries and years used in this study are based on censuses collected between 1960 and 2015. Individual migrants can be identified as people who have changed residence across a major administrative unit during the year prior, or five years prior, to the census date. Thus, the analysis is only examining the dynamics of domestic migrants.

Subnational rainfall shocks in the potential migrants' "place of origin" (that is, where they lived prior to migrating or not migrating) are also included in this set of covariates as indicators of water stress. These subnational rainfall shocks are measured by periods of low rainfall relative to long-run averages in each administrative unit.

box continues next page

BOX 1.5: Harnessing the Power of Machine Learning *continued*

Depending on the migration interval defined in each census (place of residence 1 year, 5 years, or 10 years preceding the census), corresponding climatic conditions were calculated based on the length of the migration period and an additional two years prior, that is, 3 years, 7 years, or 12 years prior to the census, respectively.

Random forest models. The analysis compares the influence of rainfall shocks on migration relative to other well-known determinants to see just how important water is for predicting migration. The size of the data set (nearly half a billion records) renders standard statistical methods intractable. Regression models have the advantage of quantifying relationships between variables of interest in a custom and interpretable way, for example, beta coefficients that allow statements about the magnitude (size of the coefficient) and relevance (significance level) of the relationship. However, very large sample sizes impede an application of regression models. Instead, the analysis relies on random forest models. Classification techniques in machine learning techniques, such as random forests, do not rely on variances and are applicable on larger samples. This nonparametric technique allows one to identify patterns and salient variables in large-scale and complex datasets without imposing any statistical assumptions. Furthermore, random forests come with a data purity metric that allows one to compare the influence of different variables.

Because random forests are an ensemble method, they are made up of a large number of small decision trees, which each produce their own predictions. The individual decision trees apply a systematic truncation of a data sample with regard to the distribution of an outcome variable (target feature). The target feature (which is analogous to a regression's dependent variable and indicates what the model is attempting to predict) in this case is whether or not an individual migrated, while the other demographic and water indicators serve as explaining features.

The variable importance of each feature is assessed by calculating the mean decrease in Gini (MDG), which is a performance metric of the random forest model. The MDG calculates by how much the performance of the model would deteriorate if a respective feature was to be excluded from the model. With MDGs for all features at hand, the relative MDG, called the "explanatory power" in figure 1.2, can be calculated for each feature. This value assesses the importance of a given feature relative to the average importance of the other features. In the figure, the value is calculated relative to the MDG of the education feature (relative MDG = MDG of feature A / MDG of education × 100). An explanatory power of more than 100 indicates that a given feature is more relevant for explaining the target feature than education on average.

Future extensions of this study could explore alternative machine learning methods, such as support vector machines, that are well suited for truncating high-dimensional feature spaces that involve many features and could combine them with inferential statistics like regression analysis.

The assessment is based on data from 442 million individual records in 1,392 regions across 64 countries and 189 censuses spanning the period from 1960 to 2015. This is the largest data set on internal migrants ever assembled. Migration data from these individual records are combined with climate data on the occurrence of dry rainfall shocks—as measured by periods of low rainfall relative to long-run averages—in the potential migrants' place of origin. This measure of water stress is then used to test the influence of water on migration relative to standard well-known migration indicators, such as age, gender, education, marital status, and the number of people living in the household.

Age, gender, and education are considered the top three sources of observable heterogeneity in population studies (Lutz 2014). Because migration is not a random process, migrants are often selected on the basis of these characteristics. Consistencies in the age patterns of migrants are well documented in comparisons with gender and education dimensions. Migration rates are generally higher in early adulthood and lower upon exit from the labor market (Rogers and Castro 1981; Bernard, Bell, and Charles-Edwards 2014; Bernard and Bell 2015). But there are scarce empirical regularities in gendered patterns of migration. On the one hand, if women are more vulnerable to water shocks than men, the stronger impact of water shocks on their livelihoods could trigger migration as an adaptation response. On the other hand, women may have lower ability to use migration as an adaptation option, especially if they have lower opportunities in the labor market compared to men (Chindarkar 2012; Cattaneo et al. 2019; Afridi, Mahajan and Sangwan 2021). Similarly, there is no conclusive evidence on whether migrants are drawn from a pool of less or more educated individuals. Empirical studies show that educational-level selectivity differs across countries and individuals (Gould 1982; Quinn and Rubb 2005; Cattaneo 2007). Whether highly educated individuals are more or less likely to migrate following climatic shocks also depends on their adaptive capacity and the adaptation options available.

The absence of empirical regularity regarding how demographic factors drive migration is partly due to the variation in geographic areas studied. For internal migration, in particular, large-scale cross-national studies on drivers of migration are limited. Machine learning applied to data from half a billion individual records can offer a unique opportunity to explore the predictive power of demographic characteristics and environmental factors in explaining migration outcomes across time and space.

Results are presented as a "horse race" in figure 1.2. The analysis compares the influence of rainfall shocks on migration relative to other demographic determinants to examine how important water is for predicting migration (see box 1.4). To ease interpretation, each dot in figure 1.2 shows the importance of a respective characteristic for explaining migration in a given country, relative to the importance that a demographic characteristic such as education has, on average, across all countries (100 = dotted line). A value of 200, for example, means that, in a given country, the characteristic

FIGURE 1.2: **The Importance of Water Shocks in Explaining Migration**

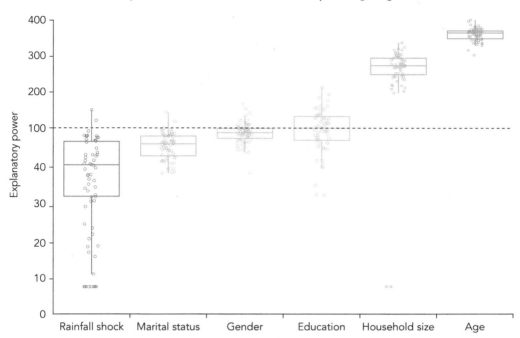

Source: World Bank figure based on data from 189 different censuses and weather data from Matsuura and Willmott 2018.
Note: The graph above summarizes the results of 189 estimates derived using random forest techniques to show the importance of various characteristics at explaining migration behavior. These estimates include data from 442 million individuals in 64 countries between 1960 and 2015. Each dot represents the results from a different country/year. The y-axis shows how critical each variable along the x-axis is for explaining migration in that country/year. The candlestick chart shows the mean for all country estimates (central bar) and the 95 percent confidence interval (outer square). Values are normalized with respect to education, such that the mean value of education takes a value of 100, and all other countries are shown relative to education's explanatory power, with values over (under) 100 implying that the value is more (less) important for explaining migration patterns.

is twice as important or relevant as education when explaining migration. A clear difference in explanatory power across characteristics is detected. Not surprisingly, age and household size are, on average, more important than education and have the largest explanatory power for regional out-migration. Other characteristics, such as gender or marital status, are, on average, as relevant as education. This is of little surprise, as the five individual characteristics are known to be relevant drivers of migration.

Notably, water shocks also can wield a considerably large influence on migration outcomes in addition to the traditional drivers of migration. Even though the occurrence of below-average rainfall is slightly less important and is about 50 percent as important as education, the box plot in figure 1.2 shows that, in contrast to individual characteristics, the range of water's importance varies considerably, and in some countries dry rainfall shocks can be as important as gender, marital status, or even education.

This analysis provides solid evidence on the importance of water in influencing migration. The rest of the report focuses on using more specific analytic and econometric techniques to interpret the relationship between migration and water.

SOCIAL DIMENSIONS OF MIGRATION

In many cases, migration entails additional challenges and hardships for marginalized communities and individuals. Although issues of social inclusion at the intersection of water and migration are clearly important, significant data gaps mean that it is difficult to provide a quantitative global assessment of the issue. For this reason, this report does not explicitly address social inclusion and marginalization. However, *Ebb and Flow: Volume 2* (Borgomeo et al. 2021) provides a perspective on this fundamental development issue in the context of forced displacement in the Middle East and North Africa. The spotlight on the COVID-19 crisis at the end of this chapter also briefly explores the significance of social cohesion from a public health perspective.

With regard to water security for migrant populations, social exclusion can take many forms, including lower levels of water access because of physical barriers or social norms, and lower participation in decision making on the use and allocation of water within the household or community (box 1.6). As discussed in *Ebb and Flow: Volume 2,* there is evidence of individuals and communities being disadvantaged or excluded from access to water services and decision making over water resources because of disability and identity, in particular as they relate to gender. Moving forward, this report calls for improved data availability on migration choices and patterns for socially vulnerable groups in society.

STRUCTURE OF THE REPORT

The preceding results from the machine learning model reveal the predictive power of water for migration outcomes, but they are not an end in themselves. Future research should aim to disentangle the mechanisms and nuances underlying these predictions and investigate the varied interactions of water with other social, economic, and demographic processes in driving migration and the subsequent impacts. In part, that is the goal of the remainder of this report. In the chapters that follow, the report presents findings from new research on the impacts of fluctuations in water availability on mobility, the flow of human capital, and on economic growth using data-driven empirical methods. Where appropriate, this new research is presented alongside existing literature to better contextualize it and to provide additional background and information.

BOX 1.6: Social Cleavages Run Deep

Migration flows and their impacts are often gendered (Morrison, Schiff, and Sjöblom 2007). Women may face discrimination in both origin and destination locations, with evidence suggesting that gender inequality can act as both an incentive and a barrier to migration (Ruyssen and Salomone 2018). Although migration can offer new opportunities for women, it can also lead to new or increased risks. In particular, conditions of forced displacement often exacerbate gender imbalances. In these situations, women and girls face severe protection challenges and heightened risks of sexual and gender-based violence. Water-related issues can act as a channel for these heightened risks: women and girls often have to use latrine facilities with no locks and have to fetch water outside refugee camp boundaries, which increases the risk of assault (UNHCR and World Bank 2015). Among displaced Syrian women in Lebanon, lack of access to drinking water and facilities for basic hygiene, including feminine hygiene products, washing water, soap, and bathing facilities, is a key factor contributing to poor reproductive health (Masterson et al. 2014). In Gaza, lack of access to adequate sanitation services prevents women and girls from participating in other productive activities (such as attending school) (UNOCHA 2019).

For indigenous people, the decision to leave one's home is often influenced by discrimination, land tenure insecurity, and the risk of forced eviction. Like other types of migrants, indigenous people might decide to move in search of economic opportunity, higher wages, or better services. In contrast to other migrants, however, indigenous people often move because of insecure land tenure, the dispossession of their lands, and the need to escape discrimination. In Cambodia, for example, indigenous people face discrimination and coerced displacement because of illegal land evictions linked with resource extraction and deforestation (IWGIA 2018). Given their strong dependence on climate-sensitive ecosystems such as deserts and tropical forests for their mental and material well-being, indigenous people are also more vulnerable to climate variability and change and its potential impact on livelihoods. Indigenous people are also more likely to experience marginalization once they migrate to urban areas (United Nations 2018). In Latin America, indigenous migrants in urban areas are twice as likely to end up living in informal settlements with limited access to basic services, including water, compared with nonindigenous migrants (World Bank 2015).

Very little is known about the intersection of disability with migration. People with disabilities face fewer opportunities to migrate and they face additional barriers during migration and in the place of destination because of changes in the environment and the absence of services and care (for example, the layout of infrastructure in camps or settlements) (Mirza 2014). The United Nations High Commissioner for Refugees estimates that, on average, 4 percent of refugees and asylum seekers in the Middle East and North Africa have disability status (UNHCR 2019). Underidentification and underreporting of people with disabilities mean that the total number of people with disabilities who decide to, or are forced to, move from their homes is unknown (GMDAC 2016). Even less is known about the challenges they face, including those related to water.

Chapter 2 examines the link between water, migration, and development at a global scale. The chapter finds that, on average, water deficits result in five times as much migration as do water deluges, despite the fact that floods are much more likely to gain national or international attention. But there are important nuances to *why* and *when* these events lead to increased migration. The effects vary significantly based on country income, as well as people's ability to adapt to water deficits via buffering investments in gray and green infrastructure. Understanding these nuances is critical to developing strategies to help households cope with water shocks, thus easing the migration transition, and for regional development policy more generally.

Chapter 3 focuses on the person's individual characteristics and explores the role of human capital in driving the relationship between water and migration. This chapter demonstrates that water shocks can influence the *type* of workers that migrate. Workers moving out of regions with lower rainfall and frequent dry shocks bring with them lower-than-average education levels and skills. This can have profound implications for the migrants themselves as well as for the regions they move to, highlighting that adverse shocks can have economic consequences far beyond the regions they affect immediately.

Chapter 4 explores the impact of droughts on urban growth. Cities, which are most often the destination of migrants, are believed to be more resilient than rural areas to the types of water shocks that induce migration. But even in cities, water deficits can continue to haunt migrants. Recent high-profile urban droughts in Cape Town South Africa, São Paolo, Brazil, and Chennai, India, show that some of the world's megacities are increasingly beginning to face "day zero" events in which water supplies become threateningly low. Dozens of cities across the globe face similar fates of dwindling water supplies, yet they gain little attention. This report finds that water shortages can be a significant drag on economic growth in cities across the world, enough to reverse critical development progress.

Finally, chapter 5 builds on the results, analysis, and literature of this report and attempts to provide policy insights into the evolving nature of the relationship between water, migration, and development.

The technical appendix to this report, available at www.worldbank.org /ebbflow, goes into more detail on the data employed, technical details of all analyses in the report, and several analyses that are congruent to the report's findings.

REFERENCES

Adams, S., F. Baarsch, A. Bondeau, D. Coumou, R. Donner, K. Frieler, B. Hare, A. Menon, M. Perette, F. Piontek, K. Rehfeld, A. Robinson, M. Rocha, J. Rogelj, J. Runge, M. Schaeffer, J. Schewe, C. F. Schleussner, S. Schwan,

O. Serdeczny, A. Svirejeva-Hopkins, M. Vieweg, and L. Warszawski. 2013. *Turn Down the Heat: Climate Extremes, Regional Impacts, and the Case for Resilience—Full Report*. Washington, DC: World Bank.

Afridi, F., K. Mahajan, and N. Sangwan. 2021. "The Gendered Effects of Climate Change: Production Shocks and Labor Response in Agriculture." IZA Discussion Paper 14568, IZA-Institute of Labor Economics, Bonn, Germany.

Amrith. S. 2018. *Unruly Waters How Rains, Rivers, Coasts, and Seas Have Shaped Asia's History*. New York: Basic Books.

Barker, N., C. A. Davis, P. López-Peña, H. Mitchell, A. M. Mobarak, K. Naguib, M. E. Reimão, A. Shenoy, and C. Vernot. 2020. "Migration and the Labour Market Impacts of COVID-19." WIDER Working Paper 139/2020, United Nations University–World Institute for Development Economics Research, Helsinki.

Bernard, A., and M. Bell. 2015. "Smoothing Internal Migration Age Profiles for Comparative Research." *Demographic Research* 32 (1): 915–48.

Bernard, A., M. Bell, and E. Charles-Edwards. 2014. "Life-Course Transitions and the Age Profile of Internal Migration." *Population and Development Review* 40 (2): 213–39.

Bhardwaj, G., T. Esch, S. V. Lall, M. Marconcini, M. E. Soppelsa, and S. Wahba. 2020. *Cities, Crowding, and the Coronavirus: Predicting Contagion Risk Hotspots*. Washington, DC: World Bank. https://openknowledge.worldbank.org/handle/10986/33648.

Blakeslee, D., R. Fishman, and V. Srinivasan. 2020. "Way Down in the Hole: Adaptation to Long-Term Water Loss in Rural India." *American Economic Review* 110 (1): 200–24.

Blankespoor, B., A. Khan, and H. Selod. 2019. "The Two Tails of Cities. A (More) Exhaustive Perspective on Urban Population Growth and City Spatial Expansion." Unpublished manuscript.

Borgomeo, Edoardo, Anders Jägerskog, Esha Zaveri, Jason Russ, Amjad Khan, and Richard Damania. 2021. *Ebb and Flow: Volume 2. Water in the Shadow of Conflict in the Middle East and North Africa*. Washington, DC: World Bank.

Burchfield, M., H. G. Overman, D. Puga, and M. A. Turner. 2006. "Causes of Sprawl: A Portrait from Space." *Quarterly Journal of Economics* 121 (2): 587–633.

Cattaneo, C. 2007. "The Self-Selection in the Migration Process: What Can We Learn?" LIUC Papers in Economics No. 199, Carlo Cattaneo University, Castallanza, Italy.

Cattaneo, C., M. Beine, C.J. Fröhlich, D. Kniveton, I. Martinez-Zarzoso, M. Mastrorillo, K. Millock, E. Piguet, and B. Schraven. 2019. "Human Migration in the Era of Climate Change." *Review of Environmental Economics and Policy* 13 (2): 189–206.

Chen, J., and V. Mueller. 2018. "Coastal Climate Change, Soil Salinity and Human Migration in Bangladesh." *Nature Climate Change* 8 (11): 981.

Chindarkar, N. 2012. "Gender and Climate Change-Induced Migration: Proposing a Framework for Analysis." *Environmental Research Letters* 7 (2): 025601. https://doi.org/10.1088/1748-9326/7/2/025601.

Colmer, J. 2018. *Weather, Labor Reallocation and Industrial Production: Evidence from India*. LSE Research Online Documents on Economics 88695, London School of Economics and Political Science, London.

Dalgaard, C.-J., A. S. B. Knudsen, and P. Selaya. 2020. "The Bounty of the Sea and Long-Run Development." *Journal of Economic Growth* 25 (3): 259–95.

Damania, R., S. Desbureaux, M. Hyland, A. Islam, S. Moore, A.-S. Rodella, J. Russ, and E. Zaveri. 2017. *Uncharted Waters: The New Economics of Water Scarcity and Variability*. Washington, DC: World Bank.

Emerick, K. 2018. "Agricultural Productivity and the Sectoral Reallocation of Labor in Rural India." *Journal of Development Economics* 135: 488–503.

Fishman, R., M. Jain, and A. Kishore. 2017. "When Water Runs Out: Scarcity, Adaptation, and Migration in Gujarat." International Growth Center working paper, London School of Economics and Political Science, London.

GMDAC (Global Migration Data Analysis Centre). 2016. *GMDAC Data Briefing: Disability and Unsafe Migration: Data and Policy, Understanding the Evidence*. Geneva: International Organization for Migration.

Gollin, D., S. Parente, and R. Rogerson. 2002. "The Role of Agriculture in Development." *American Economic Review* 92 (2): 160–64.

Gould, W. T. S. 1982. "Education and Internal Migration: A Review and Report." *International Journal of Educational Development* 1 (3): 103–11.

Gupta, A. K., D. M. Anderson, D. N. Pandey, and A. K. Singhvi. 2006. "Adaptation and Human Migration, and Evidence of Agriculture Coincident with Changes in the Indian Summer Monsoon during the Holocene." *Current Science* 90: 1082–90.

Hall, J. W., D. Grey, D. Garrick, F. Fung, C. Brown, S. J. Dadson, and C. W. Sadoff. 2014. "Coping with the Curse of Freshwater Variability." *Science* 346 (6208): 429–30.

Harris, J., and M. P. Todaro. 1970. "Migration, Unemployment, and Development: A Two Sector Analysis." *American Economic Review* 60: 126–42.

Henderson, J. V., A. Storeygard, and U. Deichmann. 2017. "Has Climate Change Driven Urbanization in Africa?" *Journal of Development Economics* 124: 60–82.

Hoffmann, R., A. Dimitrova, R. Muttarak, J. C. Cuaresma, and J. Peisker. 2020. "A Meta-Analysis of Country-Level Studies on Environmental Change and Migration." *Nature Climate Change* 10 (10): 904–12.

Hsieh, C. T., and P. J. Klenow. 2010. "Development Accounting." *American Economic Journal: Macroeconomics* 2 (1): 207–23.

IWGIA (International Work Group for Indigenous Affairs). 2018. *The Indigenous World 2018*. Copenhagen: IWGIA. https://www.iwgia.org/images/documents/indigenous-world/indigenous-world-2018.pdf.

Jägerskog, A., and A. Swain. 2016. "Water, Migration and How They Are Interlinked." Working Paper 27, Stockholm International Water Institute, Stockholm.

Joint Data Center on Forced Displacement, World Bank Group, UNHCR (United Nations High Commissioner for Refugees). 2020. *Compounding Misfortunes: Changes in Poverty Since the Onset of COVID-19 on Syrian*

Refugees and Host Communities in Jordan, the Kurdistan Region of Iraq and Lebanon (English). Washington, DC: World Bank Group.

Lagakos, D. 2020. "Urban–Rural Gaps in the Developing World: Does Internal Migration Offer Opportunities?" *Journal of Economic Perspectives* 34 (3): 174–92.

Lehmann, J., F. Mempel, and D. Coumou. 2018. "Increased Occurrence of Record-Wet and Record-Dry Months Reflect Changes in Mean Rainfall." *Geophysical Research Letters* 45 (24): 13468–76.

Lewis, A. 1954. "Economic Development with Unlimited Supplies of Labour." *Manchester School of Economic and Social Studies* 22: 139–91.

Lutz, W. 2014. "A Population Policy Rationale for the Twenty-First Century." *Population and Development Review* 40 (3): 527–44.

Masterson, A. R., J. Usta, J. Gupta, and A. S. Ettinger. 2014. "Assessment of Reproductive Health and Violence Against Women among Displaced Syrians in Lebanon." *BMC Women's Health* 14 (1): 1–8.

Matsurra, K., and C. J. Willmott. 2018. "Terrestrial Air Temperature and Precipitation: Monthly and Annual Time Series (1900–2017)." http://climate.geog.udel.edu/~climate/html_pages/download.html.

McAuliffe, M., and M. Ruhs. 2017. *World Migration Report 2018*. Geneva: International Organization for Migration.

Michaels, G., F. Rauch, and S. J. Redding. 2012. "Urbanization and Structural Transformation." *Quarterly Journal of Economics* 127 (2): 535–86.

Millock, K. 2015. "Migration and Environment." *Annual Review of Resource Economics* 7 (1): 35–60.

Minnesota Population Center. 2019. Integrated Public Use Microdata Series, International: Version 4.2 [dataset]. University of Minnesota, Minneapolis. https://doi.org/10.18128/D020.V7.2.

Mirza, M. 2014. "Disability and Forced Migration." In *The Oxford Handbook of Refugee and Forced Migration Studies*, 1–10. Oxford: Oxford University Press.

Morrison, A. R., M. Schiff, and M. Sjöblom. 2007. *The International Migration of Women*. Washington, DC: World Bank and Palgrave Macmillan.

Pokhrel, Y., F. Felfelani, Y. Satoh, J. Boulange, P. Burek, A. Gädeke, D. Gerten, S. N. Gosling, M. Grillakis, L. Gudmundsson, N. Hanasaki, H. Kim, A. Koutroulis, J. Liu, L. Papadimitriou, J. Schewe, H. Müller Schmied, T. Stacke, C.-E. Telteu, W. Thiery, T. Veldkamp, F. Zhao, and Y. Wada. 2021. "Global Terrestrial Water Storage and Drought Severity under Climate Change." *Nature Climate Change* 11: 226–33.

Preobrazhensky, E. 1921. *The Crisis of Soviet Industrialization* (1980 edition). London: MacMillan.

Quinn, M. A., and S. Rubb. 2005. "The Importance of Education-Occupation Matching in Migration Decisions." *Demography* 42 (1): 153–67.

Ratha, D., S. De, E. J. Kim, S. Plaza, G. Seshan, and N. D. Yameogo. 2020. "Migration and Development Brief 33: Phase II: COVID-19 Crisis through a Migration Lens." KNOMAD-World Bank, Washington, DC.

Restuccia, D., and R. Rogerson. 2017. "The Causes and Costs of Misallocation." *Journal of Economic Perspectives* 31 (3): 151–74.

Rigaud, K. K., B. Jones, J. Bergmann, V. Clement, K. Ober, J. Schewe, S. Adamo, B. McCusker, S. Heuser, and A. Midgley. 2018. *Groundswell: Preparing for Internal Climate Migration*. Washington, DC: World Bank.

Rogers, A., and L. J. Castro. 1981. "Model Migration Schedules." IIASA Research Report (Vol. 81). International Institute for Applied Systems Analysis, Laxenburg, Austria.

Rosenstein-Rodan, P. N. 1943. "Problems of Industrialisation of Eastern and South-Eastern Europe." *Economic Journal* 53 (210/211): 202–11.

Rostow, W. W. 1960. *The Stages of Economic Growth: A Non-Communist Manifesto.* Cambridge: Cambridge University Press.

Ruyssen, I., and S. Salomone. 2018. "Female Migration: A Way Out of Discrimination?" *Journal of Development Economics* 130: 224–41.

Sarhadi, A., M. C. Ausín, M. P. Wiper, D. Touma, and N. S. Diffenbaugh. 2018. "Multidimensional Risk in a Nonstationary Climate: Joint Probability of Increasingly Severe Warm and Dry Conditions." *Science Advances* 4 (11): eaau3487.

Tombe, T., and X. Zhu. 2019. "Trade, Migration, and Productivity: A Quantitative Analysis of China." *American Economic Review* 109 (5): 1843–72.

United Nations. 2018. "Indigenous Peoples and Ethnic Minorities: Marginalization Is the Norm." In *Promoting Inclusion through Social Protection: Report on the World Social Situation 2018*, 97–108. New York: United Nations.

UNHCR (United Nations High Commissioner for Refugees). 2019. *Power of Inclusion: Mapping the Protection Responses for Persons with Disabilities Among Refugees in the Middle East and North Africa Region.* Geneva: UNHCR.

UNHCR (United Nations High Commissioner for Refugees) and World Bank. 2015. *Forced Displacement and Mixed Migration in the Horn of Africa.* Geneva: UNHCR; Washington, DC: World Bank.

UNOCHA (United Nations Office for the Coordination of Humanitarian Affairs). 2019. Humanitarian Needs Overview. New York: UNOCHA

Weiss, D. 1995. "Ibn Khaldun on Economic Transformation." *International Journal of Middle East Studies* 27 (1): 29–37.

World Bank. 2015. *Latinoamérica Indígena en el Siglo XXI.* Washington, DC: World Bank.

World Bank. 2018. *Moving for Prosperity: Global Migration and Labor Markets.* Policy Research Report. Washington, DC: World Bank.

World Bank. 2021. *Global Economic Prospects, January 2021.* Washington, DC: World Bank.

World Bank. Forthcoming. *An EPIC Response: Innovative Governance for Flood and Drought Risk Management.*

Wrathall, D. J., J. Hoek, A. Walters, and A. Devenish. 2018. "*Water Stress and Human Migration: A Global, Georeferenced Review of Empirical Research.*" FAO land and water discussion paper, Food and Agriculture Organization of the United Nations, Rome.

POTLIGHT

INEQUALITY, SOCIAL COHESION, AND THE COVID-19 PUBLIC HEALTH CRISIS AT THE NEXUS OF WATER AND MIGRATION

The fallout from the COVID-19 pandemic has disrupted all aspects of social, economic, and political life, and it will inevitably influence the nexus of water and migration. But how it will do so is difficult, if not impossible, to predict. A very high degree of uncertainty remains about how long the pandemic will last, when vaccines will be successfully rolled out globally, and what the scale of the pandemic's health and economic impacts will be.

The immediate impacts of the outbreak, and the nonpharmaceutical interventions taken by governments to contain it, have disrupted travel and brought life in dense cities to a standstill. These effects have had immediate consequences for the flow of migrants, their livelihoods, and the welfare of their families. For instance, the sudden reduction in access to jobs and remittances has been found to disproportionately affect migrant households in Bangladesh and Nepal; these households experienced 25 percent declines in earnings and a fourfold increase in food insecurity (Barker et al. 2020).

Also, necessarily, the pandemic will have many medium- and longer-term effects. It will leave lasting scars on investment levels, remittance flows, the skills and health of millions who are unemployed, human capital outcomes of children (through school closures), and supply chains (World Bank 2020). All of these channels, and others, stand at the interface of water and migration, some more obviously than others. Lessons from history suggest that effects can lead to persistent losses as well:

neighborhoods affected by the contamination of their water supplies during the cholera outbreak of 1854 in London, for instance, lost property values that persisted for up to 160 years (Ambrus, Field, and Gonzalez 2020).

To limit the scope of the discussion in this chapter, the spotlight focuses on compiling recent and historical evidence on the interplay between disease outbreaks, public health, and social cohesion, with a focus on the inclusion and integration of migrants. The assimilation of migrants and other excluded groups in their host communities has consequences for inequality, productivity, and even asset values, for instance in the form of house prices. Baseline conditions such as social cohesion and inequality are affected by infectious disease outbreaks and in turn also affect communities' susceptibility to infectious diseases, behavioral responses, and socioeconomic outcomes (Bloom, Kuhn, and Prettner 2020; Jedwab et al. 2021).

Resilience to disasters and crisis situations is intricately tied to social cohesion. Over the centuries, recurrent pandemics and epidemics have occurred alongside improvements in scientific knowledge that have helped civilization adapt and build resilience to the threat of such disasters. But collective well-being requires inclusivity, especially in the case of highly infectious diseases such as COVID-19, in which the nature of externalities necessitates the inclusion of groups from all backgrounds in the policy response to be successful. This includes minority groups, migrant communities, and the residents of slums and informal settlements. Today, universal health coverage, alongside free access to essential health products such as vaccines, antimalarial bed nets, and clean water, is widely accepted as a cost-effective way to reduce the disease burden in developing countries (Jamison et al. 2018). Having anyone left behind risks the failure of all efforts to curb the disease. And as the world builds back better, ensuring equality and inclusivity of groups will be integral to resilient recovery and protection from collective threats.

WATER, PUBLIC HEALTH, AND INCLUSION

Unequivocally, the role of infrastructure and investment in the water sector is found to be central to combating disease. Six hundred years ago, Ibn Khaldun claimed that the decline of civilization arises when deterioration of sanitary conditions leads to the emergence of diseases and epidemics in cities, eventually accompanied by famine (Weiss 1995). Today, scientists and policy makers recognize more intricately how the appropriate design, management, and provision of water, sanitation, and hygiene infrastructures are the most fundamental public health investments to build the resilience of increasingly dense cities to disease and to sustain their growth (Banerjee and Duflo 2007; Ferriman 2007; Lall and Deichmann 2010; Duranton and Puga 2020).

In particular, COVID-19 has highlighted the challenges stemming from preexisting inequalities, such as differences in access to water and to sanitation for hygiene, especially among excluded groups such as migrant populations. For instance, in the developing world, residents of informal settlements that are characterized by crowding and by shared water sources and sanitation facilities find themselves in hot spots for contagion and vulnerability (Bhardwaj et al. 2020). Even in developed countries, racial and ethnic minority groups today are disproportionately affected by COVID-19 as a result of poverty, inequality, and discrimination.

The COVID-19 pandemic has also highlighted how prosocial individual behaviors add up to provide systemic benefits and protection against collective threats. The mass adoption of behaviors such as social distancing, wearing masks, and washing hands is at the core of controlling the spread of the disease and the risks posed by it. At the same time, the support of public policies is necessary to create an enabling environment and promote good practices. This support requires not only ensuring access to water, sanitation, and hygiene, but also promoting the adoption of good hygiene practices through information and education. Experiences from the water sector on the promotion of handwashing and the elimination of open defecation provide potent examples of the approaches that may prove successful. Other evidence suggests how self-targeting from the provision of free monthly coupons can be the most cost-effective approach to promoting adoption of health supplies, such as water treatment solutions (Dupas et al. 2020). Cultural differences and beliefs can prove obstacles to such campaigns. Belief in traditional medicine in Pakistan, for instance, is found to be an impediment to the uptake of hand hygiene practices, even when information campaigns are conducted (Bennett, Naqvi, and Schmidt 2018). Often, however, differences in health behavior and outcomes between cultural groups reflect underlying inequalities, such as disadvantages in education, place of residence, and access to public services (Geruso and Spears 2018; Adukia et al. 2020). Lessons such as these from the water sector have direct implications for COVID-19 containment efforts.

Diversity, when accompanied by exclusion and inequality, can also prove to be an impediment to coordination and the provision of collective goods, such as the maintenance of housing quality or the provision of water and sanitation infrastructures (Alesina, Baqir, and Easterly 1999; Algan, Hémet, and Laitin 2016). Native populations in regions that experience inflows of migrants or refugees have been found to have stronger anti-immigrant sentiments (Dustmann, Vasiljeva, and Piil Damm 2019; Tabellini 2020). The sources of such sentiments are found to be the result of competition over scarce resources, such as low-skilled immigrants crowding out local employment opportunities or putting pressure on public goods and services (Card, Dustmann, and Preston 2012; Halla, Wagner, and Zweimüller 2017). For instance, evidence from Brazil suggests that rich localities employ exclusionary regulations and reduce access to basic services for informal neighborhoods to dissuade the settlement of low-income migrants (Feler and Henderson 2011).

PANDEMICS, INEQUALITY, AND SOCIAL COHESION IN HISTORY

Historical lessons from past pandemics and epidemics also point to important policy lessons regarding the interplay between poverty, inequality, and social cohesion during such crises. The Black Death of 1347–52 led to the mass persecution of Jewish populations in Europe (Voigtländer and Voth 2012; Jedwab, Johnson, and Koyama 2019). The cholera, smallpox, and plague riots of the nineteenth century and the Ebola outbreaks of the twentieth century led to violent attacks against health and government officials. There is also some suggestive evidence that higher influenza mortality in 1918 led to a higher share of votes going to extremist parties in Germany in the 1930s (Blickle 2020). Other outbreaks—plague recurrences after the Black Death, syphilis, and HIV—led to milder forms of conflict whereby minority groups were blamed for disease outbreaks, which led to cases of medicalized prejudice, discrimination, and individual cases of targeted violence. Some historical episodes of disease outbreak gave rise to conflict and scapegoating of minority groups, while others improved social cohesion and increased cooperation. The trajectory a society takes after such disease outbreaks depends largely on the prevailing economic, social, and political context; the state of scientific knowledge; and the spread of information.

For instance, the sheer scale and devastating impact of the Black Death made some contemporaries believe it was part of a grand conspiracy (Nohl 1924; Horrox 1994). In parts of Europe, a lack of medical understanding of the disease eventually led to the plague being attributed to the poisoning of wells by Jews, which led to mass expulsions and murders. Those people most vulnerable to the disease may also become a target of grievances if they are seen as a source of spread. For instance, there is evidence of increased discrimination against African migrants during the HIV crisis (for example, Edelstein, Koser, and Heymann 2014) and the Ebola crisis (for example, Lin et al. 2015).

Indeed, today, media reports suggest an increase in discrimination against people of Asian descent in the United States (Tavernise and Oppel Jr. 2020; Petri and Slotnik 2021) and in the rest of the world (Human Rights Watch 2020) because the first known infections of the virus were found in China. Increased discrimination has also been documented against minority religious groups in South Asia (Ellis-Petersen and Rahman 2020; Human

Rights Watch 2020; Qazi 2020) and against people of African origin in Chinese cities (Burke, Akinwotu, and Kuo 2020). In general, migrants have been blamed for being "super spreaders" because they travel significant distances to find work, they are more likely to become infected, and they are at higher risk of being carriers of infection when they return (Ahsan et al. 2020; Khanna, Kochhar, and Zaveri 2020).

The prevalence of inequality and intergroup dynamics have an important role in determining whether pandemics lead to social unrest. Studies suggest that inequality between groups can lead to conflict if it causes grievances or incentivizes groups to organize and engage in conflict (Kanbur 2007; Blattman and Miguel 2010). Grievances can also be exploited by political actors to obtain gains by violent means, and ethnic identity can serve as "a strategic basis for coalitions that seek a larger share of economic or political power" (Ray and Esteban 2017). Jews served as moneylenders and tax collectors, thus resentment against them possibly existed prior to the Black Death and was only inflamed by it. Similarly, reports of discrimination against minority groups and immigrants in the aftermath of the COVID-19 epidemic come against the backdrop of a global increase in populist sentiments that predates the pandemic.

Medical understanding and beliefs about diseases determined how societies responded to past pandemics. Poison became a major form of killing in the medieval and Renaissance periods (Wexler 2017) because the Islamic Golden Age (eighth to fourteenth centuries) contributed to major advances in pharmacology (Hadžović 1997). Thus, it is not surprising that epidemics during this period became increasingly associated with accusations of poisoning. Despite technological advancement and improved scientific understanding, inequalities in education and in access to new technologies can give rise to social conflict. After the germ theory of disease became more established by the 1850s, some epidemics led to the scapegoating of disease *victims*. In the case of the smallpox epidemics of the nineteenth century, a vaccine already existed in 1796 (Wolfe and Sharp 2002). Victims were found among the poor and were seen by the elite as "guilty" for their infection, either because of their ignorance or because of their lack of consideration for the rest of society. Likewise, when a treatment became available for syphilis in 1910, women who still had syphilis came to be seen as "guilty."

Scapegoating is not necessarily restricted to religious or ethnic groups. Violent "cholera riots" took place in many cities of various industrializing nations throughout the nineteenth century (Cohn 2012, 2017). Cholera disproportionately killed the urban poor in congested nineteenth-century industrial cities in a context that was already dominated by a constant and violent class struggle between the bourgeoisie and the proletariat. In this context, the population believed that "elites with physicians as their agents had invented the disease to cull populations of the poor" (Cohn 2018).

THE MARCH FORWARD

As human settlements continue to expand and become denser to cater to expanding populations, they will increase collective exposure to emerging infectious diseases (Jones et al. 2008; Hassell et al. 2017). The contagious spread of a zoonotic virus during the current crisis has laid bare the myriad inequalities in human development, and put a spotlight on how social and planetary imbalances reinforce each other (UNDP 2020). At the same time, COVID-19 has given the world an opportunity to build back better by taking the lessons learned from this pandemic to tackle worsening inequalities and planetary pressures as progress continues to be made toward further economic and human development.

REFERENCES

Adukia, A., M. Alsan, K. Babiarz, J. D. Goldhaber-Fiebert, and L. Prince. 2020. *Religion and Sanitation Practices*. Washington, DC: World Bank.

Ahsan, R., K. Iqbal, M. Khan, A. Mushfiq Mobarak, and A. Abu Shonchoy. 2020. "Using Migration Patterns to Predict COVID-19 Risk Exposure in Developing Countries." Policy Brief, Yale Research Initiative on Innovation and Scale, Yale University, New Haven, CT.

Alesina, A., R. Baqir, and W. Easterly. 1999. "Public Goods and Ethnic Divisions." *Quarterly Journal of Economics* 114 (4): 1243–84.

Algan, Y., C. Hémet, and D. D. Laitin. 2016. "The Social Effects of Ethnic Diversity at the Local Level: A Natural Experiment with Exogenous Residential Allocation." *Journal of Political Economy* 124 (3): 696–733.

Ambrus, A., E. Field, and R. Gonzalez. 2020. "Loss in the Time of Cholera: Long-Run Impact of a Disease Epidemic on the Urban Landscape." *American Economic Review* 110 (2): 475–525.

Banerjee, A. V., and E. Duflo. 2007. "The Economic Lives of the Poor." *Journal of Economic Perspectives* 21 (1): 141–68.

Barker, N., C. A. Davis, P. López-Peña, H. Mitchell, A. M. Mobarak, K. Naguib, M. E. Reimão, A. Shenoy, and C. Vernot. 2020. "Migration and the Labour Market Impacts of COVID-19." WIDER Working Paper 139/2020. United Nations University–World Institute for Development Economics Research, Helsinki.

Bennett, D., A. Naqvi, and W. P. Schmidt. 2018. "Learning, Hygiene and Traditional Medicine." *Economic Journal* 128 (612): F545–74.

Bhardwaj, G., T. Esch, S. V. Lall, M. Marconcini, M. E. Soppelsa, and S. Wahba. 2020. *Cities, Crowding, and the Coronavirus: Predicting Contagion Risk Hotspots*. Washington, DC: World Bank. https://openknowledge.worldbank.org/handle/10986/33648.

Blattman, C., and E. Miguel. 2010. "Civil War." *Journal of Economic Literature* 48 (1): 3–57.

Blickle, K. 2020. *Pandemics Change Cities: Municipal Spending and Voter Extremism in Germany, 1918–1933*. Staff Report No. 921, Federal Reserve Bank of New York.

Bloom, D. E., M. Kuhn, and K. Prettner. 2020. *Modern Infectious Diseases: Macroeconomic Impacts and Policy Responses*. Cambridge, MA: National Bureau of Economic Research.

Burke, J., E. Akinwotu, and L. Kuo. 2020. "China Fails to Stop Racism Against Africans over Covid-19." *Guardian*, April 27.

Card, D., C. Dustmann, and I. Preston. 2012. "Immigration, Wages, and Compositional Amenities." *Journal of the European Economic Association* 10 (1): 78–119.

Cohn, S. K. 2012. "Pandemics: Waves of Disease, Waves of Hate from the Plague of Athens to A.I.D.S." *Historical Journal* 85 (230): 535–55.

Cohn, S. K. 2017. "Cholera Revolts: A Class Struggle We May Not Like." *Social History* 42 (2): 162–80.

Cohn, S. K. 2018. *Epidemics: Hate and Compassion from the Plague of Athens to AIDS*. Oxford: Oxford University Press.

Dupas, P., B. Nhlema, Z. Wagner, A. Wolf, and E. Wroe. 2020. *Expanding Access to Clean Water for the Rural Poor: Experimental Evidence from Malawi*. Cambridge, MA: National Bureau of Economic Research.

Duranton, G., and D. Puga. 2020. "The Economics of Urban Density." *Journal of Economic Perspectives* 34 (3): 3–26.

Dustmann, C., K. Vasiljeva, and A. Piil Damm. 2019. "Refugee Migration and Electoral Outcomes." *Review of Economic Studies* 86 (5): 2035–91.

Edelstein, M., K. Koser, and D. L. Heymann. 2014. "Health Crises and Migration." In *Humanitarian Crises and Migration*, 97–112. London: Routledge.

Ellis-Petersen, H., and S. A. Rahman. 2020. "How Lives Were Destroyed under Cover of Lockdown in a Small Indian Town." *Guardian*, June 8.

Feler, L., and J. V. Henderson. 2011. "Exclusionary Policies in Urban Development: Under-servicing Migrant Households in Brazilian Cities." *Journal of Urban Economics* 69 (3): 253–72.

Ferriman, A. 2007. "BMJ Readers Choose the 'Sanitary Revolution' As Greatest Medical Advance Since 1840." *BMJ* 334: 111.

Geruso, M., and D. Spears. 2018. "Neighborhood Sanitation and Infant Mortality." *American Economic Journal: Applied Economics* 10 (2): 125–62.

Hadžović, S. 1997. "Farmacija i veliki doprinos Arapske islamske znanosti u njenom razvitku" ["Pharmacy and the Great Contribution of Arab-Islamic Science to Its Development"]. *Medicinski Arhiv* 51 (1–2): 47–50.

Halla, M., A. F. Wagner, and J. Zweimüller. 2017. "Immigration and Voting for the Far Right." *Journal of the European Economic Association* 15 (6): 1341–85.

Hassell, J. M., M. Begon, M. J. Ward, and E. M. Fèvre. 2017. "Urbanization and Disease Emergence: Dynamics at the Wildlife–Livestock–Human Interface." *Trends in Ecology and Evolution* 32 (1): 55–67.

Horrox, R. 1994. *The Black Death*. Manchester: Manchester University Press.

Human Rights Watch. 2020. *Covid-19 Fueling Anti-Asian Racism and Xenophobia Worldwide*. New York: Human Rights Watch.

Jamison, D. T., A. Alwan, C. N. Mock, R. Nugent, D. Watkins, O. Adeyi, S. Anand, R. Atun, S. Bertozzi, Z. Bhutta, and A. Binagwaho. 2018. "Universal

Health Coverage and Intersectoral Action for Health: Key Messages from Disease Control Priorities." *Lancet* 391 (10125): 1108–20.

Jan, T. 2020. "Asian American Doctors and Nurses Are Fighting Racism and the Coronavirus." *Washington Post*, May 20.

R., N. D. Johnson, and M. Koyama. 2019. "Negative Shocks and Mass Persecutions: Evidence from the Black Death." *Journal of Economic Growth* 24 (4): 345–95.

Jedwab, R., A. M. Khan, J. Russ, and E. D. Zaveri. 2021. "Epidemics, Pandemics, and Social Conflict: Lessons from the Past and Possible Scenarios for COVID-19." World Development. doi: https://doi.org/10.1016/j.worlddev.2021.105629.

Jones, K. E., N. G. Patel, M. A. Levy, A. Storeygard, D. Balk, J. L. Gittleman, and P. Daszak. 2008. "Global Trends in Emerging Infectious Diseases." *Nature* 451 (7181): 990–93.

Kanbur, R. 2007. "Poverty, Inequality and Conflict." Working Paper No. 126997. Cornell University, Department of Applied Economics and Management, Ithaca, NY.

Khanna, M., N. Kochhar, and E. Zaveri. 2020. "Ensuring Safety of Migrants Key Policy Challenge for Govt." *Hindustan Times*, May 9.

Lall, S. V., and U. Deichmann. 2010. *Density and Disasters: Economics of Urban Hazard Risk*. Washington, DC: World Bank.

Lin, L., B. J. Hall, L. C. Khoe, A. B. Bodomo, and M. A. Rothstein. 2015. "Ebola Outbreak: From the Perspective of African Migrants in China." *American Journal of Public Health* 105 (5): E5.

Nohl, Johannes. 1924. *The Black Death: A Chronicle of the Plague*. George Allen and Unwin.

Petri, A. E., and D. E. Slotnik. 2021. "Attacks on Asian-Americans in New York Stoke Fear, Anxiety and Anger." *New York Times*, February 26.

Qazi, S. 2020. "Sri Lanka: Muslims Face Extra Threat as Coronavirus Stirs Hate." *Al Jazeera*, May 11.

Ray, D., and J. Esteban. 2017. "Conflict and Development." *Annual Review of Economics* 9 (1): 263–93.

Tabellini, M. 2020. "Gifts of the Immigrants, Woes of the Natives: Lessons from the Age of Mass Migration." *Review of Economic Studies* 87 (1): 454–86.

Tavernise, S., and R. A. Oppel Jr. 2020. "Spit On, Yelled At, Attacked: Chinese-Americans Fear for Their Safety." *New York Times*, March 25.

UNDP (United Nations Development Programme). 2020. *Human Development Report 2020. The Next Frontier: Human Development and the Anthropocene*. New York: UNDP. http://www.hdr.undp.org/en/2020-report.

Voigtländer, N., and H. J. Voth. 2012. "Persecution Perpetuated: The Medieval Origins of Anti-Semitic Violence in Nazi Germany." *Quarterly Journal of Economics* 127 (3): 1339–92.

Weiss, D. 1995. "Ibn Khaldun on Economic Transformation." *International Journal of Middle East Studies* 27 (1): 29–37.

Wexler, P. 2017. *Toxicology in the Middle Ages and Renaissance*. Elsevier Science.

Wolfe, R. M., and L. K. Sharp. 2002. "Anti-vaccinationists Past and Present." *BMJ* 325 (7361): 430–32.

World Bank. 2020. *Global Economic Prospects, June 2020*. Washington, DC: World Bank.

CHAPTER TWO

STAY OR GO?

"Say goodbye to the might-have-beens . . .
You go because you must"

—**Ruth Padel,** *The Mara Crossing*

KEY HIGHLIGHTS

- This chapter presents new research to examine the link between water, migration, and development at a global scale. It finds that cumulative water shocks play a significant role in influencing migration, with water deficits resulting in five times as much migration as water deluges.

- But there are important nuances in why and when this migration occurs, and headline predictions of massive waves of "water refugees" can be misleading.

- Migration responses differ systematically between low-income and middle-income settings. Where there is extreme poverty and migration is costly, rainfall deficits are more likely to trap people than induce them to migrate.

- Buffering investments in built infrastructure (such as irrigation) or access to natural infrastructure (such as forests) can diminish the risk of water shocks, smooth income shocks, and lessen the impact of rainfall deficits on migration. But this is not true everywhere and every time.

- When irrigation induces maladaptation whereby farmers grow water-intensive crops or natural capital is depleted, causing declines in ecosystem services, their buffering services are lost. In such cases, water shocks can further accentuate vulnerability and heighten the impact of rainfall deficits on migration.

INTRODUCTION

The history of migration is sculpted by water. Confronted by harsh and prolonged dry spells in East Africa's Rift Valley over 5 million years ago, our ancestors decided to migrate and move across Africa in search of new sources of water. Scholars argue that this pivotal decision may have been key to their survival and the evolution of the human species (Cuthbert et al. 2017). Centuries later, human movement and migration have come to be recognized as one of the foundational drivers of economic development and growth. As explained in chapter 1, vast population movements from rural to urban areas and from agricultural to nonagricultural activities have been an important channel through which countries develop. By affecting movement, the availability of water has the potential to influence this process of transformation.

This chapter casts light on these development issues by investigating the relationship between water shocks and the internal migration mechanisms underlying the process of development at a global scale. The analysis uses a global and fine-grained data set spanning three decades for close to 150 countries to demonstrate the widespread nature of the effects while also uncovering significant heterogeneous impacts across different contexts. Results reveal that, overall, cumulative water deficits play a critical role in driving migration decisions. But these migration responses are conditional on income levels and notably on people's ability to adapt to and to buffer their income against water shocks via investments in hydraulic infrastructure or leveraging nature's ecosystem services or other buffering mechanisms (which might include savings from income).

These issues have far-reaching policy consequences. As economies develop, populations grow, and climate change takes hold, water shocks will pose an increasingly complex challenge to people. Scientists warn that two-thirds of Earth's land is already on track to lose water as the climate warms, with extreme-to-exceptional drought likely to affect more than double the area and population by the end of this century (Pokhrel et al. 2021). These estimates mean that nearly 700 million people, or 8 percent of the projected future population, could be affected by extreme drought, compared with 200 million over recent decades (Pokhrel et al. 2021). Understanding the uneven impacts across subsets of the population and the effectiveness of remedies that buffer incomes against water shocks will be critical to help inform the debate on future migration responses to continued climate change.

Because almost three times as many people migrate within countries than internationally, these questions are especially salient for internal migration (McAuliffe and Ruhs 2017). Past simulations project that an estimated 143 million people in Sub-Saharan Africa, South Asia, and Latin America will migrate within their own countries by 2050 in response to climatic variability (Rigaud et al. 2018). Some reports warn that massive waves of "water refugees" are likely to become commonplace as water runs out (Brown 2012). New analysis in this chapter goes beneath the headline predictions to reveal important nuances in the water–migration relationship. Understanding these nuances will be critical for designing policies to make communities more resilient and to help households cope with water shocks, thus easing the migration transition. The technical appendix to this report, available at www.worldbank.org/ebbflow, provides details of all results.

SHOULD I STAY OR SHOULD I GO? ESTIMATING THE IMPACTS OF WATER SHOCKS ON MIGRATION DECISIONS

The most straightforward question "Why did you migrate?" is perhaps the hardest to answer. Every migrant has a unique story and experience. People's choices to move, stay, or engage in local livelihoods occur within the context of a wide array of social, cultural, and economic factors and their interlinkages that can amplify or moderate the influence of water on migration.[1] But at its economic core, the decision boils down to two salient questions: Do people perceive improved welfare or wealth if they were to migrate? (the *incentive* condition); and, Can they afford to migrate? (the *feasibility* condition) (Roy 1951; Borjas 1987; Cattaneo and Peri 2015; Peri and Sasahara 2019) (see figure 2.1).

Calculus of Risks, Incentives, and Costs

There are sound economic reasons to expect successive water shocks to cascade into migration. When droughts occur, incomes suffer, especially in rural areas where agriculture remains the primary source of employment. Rural adaptation strategies, in turn, can moderate the impact of water shocks on income. Over time, water shocks can alter an individual's risk calculus of staying or leaving owing to differences in economic opportunities between where they are and where they intend to go. When their economic outlook is sufficiently high to offset the costs of moving, people may choose to move. Figure 2.1 depicts some of the channels explored in the analysis.

To systematically estimate the impacts of water shocks on internal migration, the analysis employs a subnational grid cell-level data set of net migration rates covering about 150 countries. The grid-level data for decennial net migration rates cover a 30-year time period from 1970 to 2000. This data set is combined with other fine-grained data on population, weather fluctuations, and other variables to statistically estimate the effect of rainfall shocks on migration decisions (see box 2.1 for details).

FIGURE 2.1: Main Results at a Glance: Channels through Which Rainfall Deficits Affect Migration

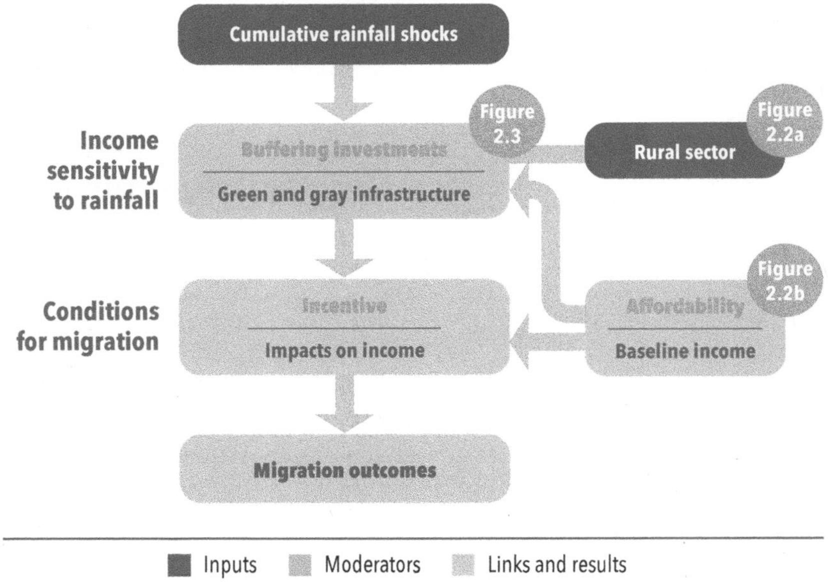

Source: World Bank figure based on analysis.

BOX 2.1: Using Disaggregated Global Data to Illuminate Water and Migration Links

Chapter 2 employs regression analysis to study the impact of rainfall variability on net migration rates using a grid cell-level data set covering the entire world. Data on net migration are drawn from the global estimated net migration data set compiled by de Sherbinin et al. (2015). To arrive at net migration estimates, the compilation begins with a gridded distribution of population in the year 2000 based on census data drawn from the Global Rural–Urban Mapping Project, Version 1. The History Database of the Global Environment, Version 3.1, is then used to calculate population totals in 1970, 1980, and 1990 to arrive at population growth estimates for previous decades. Mortality rates specific to each nation, ethnicity group, and decade are applied to each grid cell to estimate decennial births and deaths. Finally, a measure for net population growth, defined as births minus deaths plus net migration, is used to estimate the net migration for each grid cell.

Because the data set derives an aggregate measure of net migration rates from assumed demographic trends, it is not possible to account for individual specific

box continues next page

BOX 2.1: Using Disaggregated Global Data to Illuminate Water and Migration Links *continued*

data, or to distinguish between short- and long-term migration and temporary and permanent migration. Despite these limitations, the data set allows an assessment of aggregate migration trends and its links to water shocks at a granular scale. The same data set on net migration has also been employed by de Sherbinin et al. (2012) in the context of environmental research and by Peri and Sasahara (2019) to study the effect of temperature increases on net migration.

The analysis splits the land area into 0.5 degree grid cells (approximately 56 kilometers x 56 kilometers at the equator). Following Peri and Sasahara (2019), the net migration data from de Sherbinin et al. (2015) are aggregated to the 0.5 degree resolution to reduce data volatility from small cells and minimize measurement errors. This aggregation is then combined with data on population obtained from Yamagata and Murakami (2015) to construct decadal net migration rates. The final measure of migration for each grid cell reflects percentage changes in population due to mobility. Using disaggregated data is critical because rainfall tends to exhibit significant spatial variability that is almost two times higher than temperature (Damania, Desbureaux, and Zaveri 2020).[a] Using aggregated data at the country level would mask this spatial variability and cause substantial statistical distortions, biasing the results.

Rainfall variability is measured in terms of local deviations from the long-run mean and reflects random draws from a climate distribution (Dell, Jones, and Olken 2014). Specifically, a grid cell is considered to have a *dry rainfall shock* if rainfall in a given year is lower than the long-run annual mean for the grid cell by at least 1 standard deviation. Similarly, a grid cell is considered to have a *wet rainfall shock* if rainfall in a given year is higher than the long-run annual mean for the grid cell by at least 1 standard deviation. Shocks are considered to be better predictors of migration outcomes than raw climate data (Gray and Wise 2016; Mueller, Gray, and Hopping 2020). In the analysis, the rainfall shock variables measure the *number* of years in the decade for which rainfall was at least 1 standard deviation above or below the mean.

A plethora of other factors can also affect net migration rates. Control variables, including temperature and various fixed effects and time trends, are included to ensure that the impact of rainfall shocks is estimated precisely and not biased by factors that may be correlated with both net migration rates and rainfall shocks. These controls account for baseline differences in migration patterns and other factors that vary by year and decade. These factors include national trends in economic growth or common shocks that might affect all individuals' migration decisions in the same decade in a region (for example, border enforcement policies or conflict).

a. In 2000, the within-country coefficient of variation is 1.9 times as large for precipitation as it is for temperature (0.055 for precipitation versus 0.029 for temperature).

The analysis distinguishes between dry and wet rainfall shocks (defined as rainfall that is at least 1 standard deviation below or above normal levels).[2] Dry shocks indicate drier than normal conditions and wet shocks mean wetter than normal conditions. Including both measures is critical to account for nonlinearity and asymmetry in rainfall impacts. As figure 2.1 illustrates, water scarcity induced by rainfall deficits can increase an individual's incentive to migrate due to distress (the *incentive* condition described earlier). On the other hand, income-generating positive rainfall shocks that give households the ability to save can also influence migration by providing the necessary funds to migrate (the *feasibility* condition). These effects can manifest gradually as a response to cumulative changes in water variability. For this reason, the analysis focuses on the impact of repeated water shocks that occur over a decade on out-migration rates. It also suggests that focusing on a single rainfall episode may be misleading because the decision to migrate often entails high cost and longer-term considerations.

Results show strong evidence that repeated dry shocks lead to a substantial increase in out-migration. For every additional year with a dry shock, 0.3 to 0.4 percent of a grid cell's population out-migrated, on average. This amounts to dry rainfall shocks explaining between 10 and 11 percent of the increase in the out-migration rate between 1970 and 2000 across the global sample. Strikingly, dry shocks have five times the effect on out-migration than wet shocks have—the impact of wet shocks is more muted. This suggests that local adaptive capacity may be significantly constrained in the event of repeated dry shocks (Gray and Mueller 2012). But these global averages mask considerable variation in effects, which are investigated in the next section.

Pull, Push, or Trap?

Results show that out-migration effects are overwhelmingly concentrated in rural areas, where individuals are more dependent on agriculture for their income earning and sustenance (figure 2.2). For the most intensively cultivated grid cells in a country[3] (labeled "high-cropland" in figure 2.2 panel a), the effects are even stronger. For every additional year of exposure to dry shocks during the decade, an additional 1 percent of the population in cropland-intensive grid cells out-migrate, on net, an amount that is three times the effect seen in low-cropland grid cells (figure 2.2, panel a).[4] This is perhaps not surprising. Even relatively moderate rainfall deviations from long-run averages can cause large changes in crop production—dry shocks lead to as large as a 12 percent decrease in agricultural productivity per year globally (Damania et al. 2017). Thus, repeated rainfall shortfalls can adversely affect household income and accentuate deprivation through their effect on yields and livelihoods (Fishman 2016; Lesk, Rowhani, and Ramankutty 2016; Damania et al. 2017; Noack, Riekhof, and Di Falco 2019; Ibáñez, Romero, and Velásquez 2021). This, in turn, can alter an individual's decision to stay or leave.

FIGURE 2.2: Impact of Rainfall Shocks on Out-Migration Rates, by Agricultural Dependence and Income Distribution

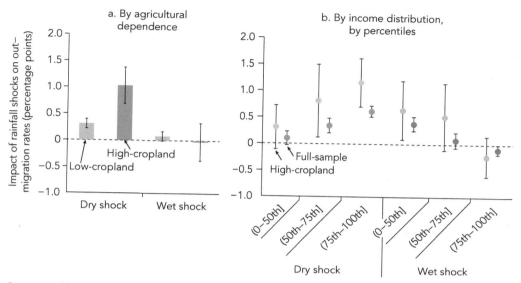

Source: World Bank figure based on analysis using global estimated net migration data by de Sherbinin et al. 2015, population data from Yamagata and Murakami 2015, cropland data from Ramankutty et al. 2008, and weather data from Matsuura and Willmott 2018.

Note: Figure 2.2 shows point estimates of an additional rainfall shock on the out-migration rate with 90 percent confidence intervals. The vertical axis shows the impact on out-migration rates in percentage points. In panel b, (0-50th], (50th-75th], and (75th-100th] denote the percentiles of the baseline income per capita distribution in the world.

What is less apparent is that these choices are also moderated by baseline differences in income or wealth. Results in figure 2.2, panel b, show that out-migration responses become stronger along an income gradient. Repeated dry shocks have little or no discernible impact on out-migration for poorer individuals residing in countries whose baseline gross domestic product (GDP) per capita falls in the bottom two quartiles of the income distribution. Yet, they also increase out-migration from higher-income areas whose baseline GDP falls in the top two quartiles.

What explains the lack of migration effect in low-income areas? At the low end of the income distribution, people may lack the resources to move—even with strong incentives to migrate—because of baseline poverty. In other words, even as repeated dry episodes increase the incentives to move and the incentive condition is met, these episodes can also limit the capacity to move such that the feasibility condition described earlier is binding. Poverty can worsen the financial constraints imposed by dry shocks. This makes migration infeasible for the most vulnerable and may cause people to remain "trapped" following adverse shocks.[5] In such cases, even the cost of bus fare or the possibility of leaving behind social support networks may pose a barrier to moving (de Sherbinin 2020).

In a first-of-its-kind experiment, researchers found that offering poor families in Bangladesh small cash payments of US$11.50 (akin to a few weeks' wages) induced a 22 percentage point increase in migration (Bryan, Chowdhury, and Mobarak 2014).[6] This finding confirms that the costs of migration are nontrivial for the poor.[7] On the other hand, in high-income areas, even as water shocks can worsen potential earnings, these shocks can strengthen the willingness of individuals to migrate and *push* people out because people can afford the costs of migration.

Supporting this argument, the analysis in the chapter finds that poorer households and individuals might need to experience a wet shock to migrate. Although panel a of figure 2.2 shows that wet rainfall shocks have little or no discernible impact on out-migration, panel b of figure 2.2 shows that there is significant underlying heterogeneity. When countries are split on the basis of their income level, a positive impact of wet rainfall shocks on out-migration is found, but only in poorer countries. In general, wet rainfall shocks tend to be beneficial for farmers. They are found to raise agricultural yields by 8 percent per year globally and positively affect various sectors of the economy (Damania et al. 2017).

This pattern suggests that migration as an adaptation strategy might be available to select people in the developing world. Upper-middle-income countries are those in which the process of structural transformation has started such that income levels are high enough to pay upfront migration costs (Peri and Sasahara 2019). But the most vulnerable people in the developing world who reside in low- and lower-middle-income countries might need to experience weather events such as wet shocks that allow them to raise the necessary funds to migrate. This is also in line with the idea that the poorer households cannot respond right away in the face of bad weather conditions—that they potentially need to save funds before migrating (Zhu and Garip 2020).

Depending on the context, various other constraints might also lead rural poor people to actively choose not to migrate, thereby nullifying the effect of water shocks on migration decisions (box 2.2). Understanding the reasons that more people do not migrate even when they could experience wage gains elsewhere is far from settled and remains an active area of debate in the literature (Lagakos 2020). Additional evidence and future research on this question in the context of water shocks will be critical for understanding the whole picture.

In sum, income remains the central pathway underlying the water shock and migration relationship. Rainfall shocks affect income, and this in turn influences migration. Because rural incomes are more sensitive to rainfall, the out-migration effect is heavily concentrated in agriculturally dependent areas. But the migration response is *not* uniform and is contingent on other factors such as income levels. Migration occurs when rural incomes suffer and fall—producing incentives to migrate—but only when the *feasibility* condition is not binding and people can afford the cost of migration (see figure 2.1).

BOX 2.2: Choosing Not to Migrate

Even as economics views the world as irrepressibly dynamic, few would dispute the notion that markets in poor countries are full of "friction." In addition to restricting budgets and making it too costly for people to migrate, rainfall shocks might deter migration in other ways.

Friction in land markets can be potent in holding back migration. In the absence of formal titles to land, people might fear losing their land, which in turn can deter migration (de Janvry et al. 2015; Chen 2017; Gottlieb and Grobovšek 2019). Informational friction too has been found to be an important barrier to migration and could also influence the water–migration relationship. In a study about migration expectations among rural Kenyans, Baseler (2019) found that even as workers in cities had the potential to earn twice as much as their rural counterparts, rural workers substantially underestimated the magnitude of this wage gap because of poor information about wages in the destination (Lagakos 2020).

People may also actively choose to stay under certain conditions. Prevailing labor market conditions and the local economy can influence the underlying incentives not to migrate. For example, a drought might increase local demand for agricultural labor due to the elevation of on-farm risk. This increase in demand for labor could lead more people to work on farms to minimize the damages to crops (Grabrucker and Grimm 2020; Jagnani et al. 2020; Mueller, Gray, and Hopping 2020). Yet another explanation could be labor reallocation to other sectors. In the presence of large firms and sufficient rural industrialization, rural poor people may be relatively successful in offsetting water-induced agricultural income losses through a reallocation of labor to off-farm employment in the same vicinity without resorting to migration (Blakeslee, Fishman, and Srinivasan 2020).

The presence of other social safety nets, such as cash transfer programs, food aid, or access to social networks, may also break the link between droughts and migration and cause people to stay. Governments can aid regions affected by natural disasters or other extreme weather events, which could dampen the economic impact of such shocks and thus influence migration. There is some suggestive evidence that food aid can delay or reduce migration (Hammond et al. 2005; Cattaneo et al. 2019; Meze-Hausken 2000). Nontraditional drought policies such as cash transfer programs can also unintentionally augment adaptive capacity and help the poor to smooth income shocks caused by droughts, thereby eliminating the incentives to move completely (Verner and Tebaldi 2015). Access to social networks also has been found to weaken the relationship between migration and rainfall deficits (Nawrotzki et al. 2015).

box continues next page

BOX 2.2: **Choosing Not to Migrate** *continued*

Various "pull" factors in potential destination regions, such as the paucity of available work and lack of a manufacturing base, can also reduce the aspiration to move (Henderson, Storeygard, and Deichmann 2017; Mueller, Gray, and Hopping 2020; Mueller et al. 2020). Moreover, the nonmonetary costs of harsh living and working conditions in the destination and the nonmonetary value of rural life may also serve as significant migration barriers for people of lower income (Imbert and Papp 2020; Lagakos 2020). Take for example the amenities that are found in large cities. These can be quite different from those in rural areas and people could have strong and varied preferences for them. In such cases, migrants could experience large welfare reductions even as their relative wages in cities rise.

DOES BUFFERING RURAL INCOME FROM RAINFALL SHOCKS INFLUENCE MIGRATION?

The previous section emphasized a rural channel in driving water-induced migration and highlighted the vital role that income plays in influencing water-induced migration. This raises a complementary question: Can rural adaptation strategies that moderate the impact of water shocks on income also influence migration? Evidence for such effects is seldom known but is essential to understand, especially in light of adaptation taking center stage in policy discussions. The Global Commission on Adaptation points to adaptation as a central factor underpinning effective responses to the impacts of climate change (Global Commission on Adaptation 2019). The analysis in this section sheds new light on these issues by examining the effect of two types of water-related adaptation mechanisms: gray hydraulic infrastructure via irrigation systems and natural green infrastructure via forest cover (figure 2.1). In doing so, this section also demonstrates how migration, as a form of adaptation, interacts with other adaptive responses to water shocks.

Liquid Assets: The Role of Hydraulic Infrastructure

From the use of aqueducts in Roman times to the modern dams and pumps of today, the control of water through irrigation systems has shaped the course of agrarian change and development of societies around the world. These supply-side measures insulate agriculture from the adverse effects of rainfall variability, shielding farmers from some of the hardships and uncertainties arising from the natural system.[8]

Prior research has shown that on average, in most areas that are equipped for irrigation, agricultural yields show limited sensitivity to rainfall variability, both for wet and dry shocks (Zaveri, Russ, and Damania 2020). This implies that irrigation infrastructure provides a buffer against rainfall shocks in these areas. For this reason, irrigation remains one of the most crucial adaptation methods used by farmers in response to risks associated with rainfall variability, and it is among the top three categories of estimated adaptation costs for developing countries (Narain, Margulis, and Essam 2011).

Yet, even as 77 percent of small-scale farms in low- and middle-income countries are located in water-scarce regions, less than a third of these have access to irrigation systems (Ricciardi et al. 2020). Low access to irrigation can become an increasingly binding constraint on agricultural livelihoods and contribute to uncertain incomes in rural areas, influencing the economic incentives underlying migration behavior. Indeed, that is what the new empirical results in this section show (box 2.3).

BOX 2.3: Measuring the Buffering Effect of Gray and Green Infrastructure

To assess the differential impacts of migration in places with low and high access to irrigation and forests, additional data sources are used. The analysis uses data on the share of irrigated cropland at the start of the period over which migration occurs (Siebert et al. 2015) and data on forest cover from the European Space Agency. These data are used to construct time-invariant shares of irrigated cropland and shares of forest cover for the sample of grid cells. Grid cells with high irrigation access and high forest access refer to those grid cells in which the baseline share of irrigated cropland or share of forested area is above the global median. The analysis follows a similar methodology to that described in box 2.1 and adds an additional interaction term between rainfall shocks and an indicator variable for high irrigation access or rainfall shocks and an indicator variable for high irrigation access. The coefficients on the interactions show the extent to which irrigation and forest access attenuate the migration response as depicted by DS × gray and DS × green in figure 2.3.

Furthermore, the analysis also examines the differential buffering impact of irrigation access in arid regions engaged in water-intensive cropping practices. The analysis combines climatic zone data along with data on the geographical distribution of agricultural crops from Ramankutty et al. (2008) to identify the crop that occupies the largest amount of harvested area in the grid cell. Grid cells whose main crops include rice, cotton, or sugarcane are identified as water-intensive grid cells.

Figure 2.3 shows the extent to which differing levels of irrigation coverage moderate water-induced out-migration (box 2.3). For example, in figure 2.3, the orange bar shows that an additional year of dry shock leads to about a 0.4 percentage point increase in net out-migration rates from areas with low access to irrigation, consistent with baseline findings in the previous section.[9] But these effects are substantially dampened in areas with high access to irrigation owing to irrigation's role in buffering and smoothing water-induced income shocks. The gray bar in figure 2.3 shows the amount of this reduction. The net effect is such that the buffering effect provided by irrigation lowers out-migration rates by about three times the rate observed in areas with low levels of irrigation coverage. Put differently, moving from the top percentile to the bottom percentile of irrigation coverage triples the impact of droughts on out-migration. Other country-level studies similarly have found that groundwater access reduces internal migration (Fishman, Jain, and Kishore 2017; Zaveri, Wrenn, and Fisher-Vanden 2020).[10] This demonstrates that the buffering role of irrigation can alter agricultural opportunity costs and reduce incentives to migrate.[11]

FIGURE 2.3: **Impact of Rainfall Shocks on Out-Migration Rates, by Gray (Irrigation) and Green (Forest) Infrastructure**

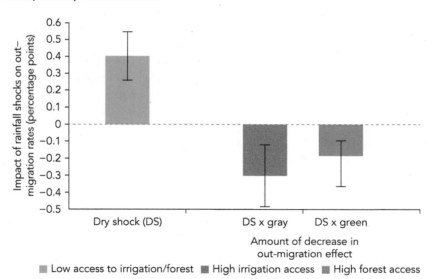

Source: World Bank figure based on analysis using global estimated net migration data by de Sherbinin et al. 2015, population data from Yamagata and Murakami 2015, irrigation data from Siebert et al. 2015, forest cover data from the European Space Agency's Climate Change Initiative, and weather data from Matsuura and Willmott 2018.
Note: Figure 2.3 shows point estimates of an additional rainfall shock on the out-migration rate with 90 percent confidence intervals. The vertical axis shows the impact on out-migration rates in percentage points. High irrigation access and high forest access refer to those grid cells where the baseline share of irrigated cropland or share of forested area is above the global median.

But even as irrigation can support agriculturally dependent communities in the short run, there are notable exceptions over the long run. Over time, irrigation systems may also paradoxically amplify the impacts of shocks in certain regions and fail to protect farmers from the impacts of droughts because of maladaptation (Hornbeck and Keskin 2014; Damania et al. 2017). In some arid areas, free irrigation water creates an illusion of abundance, which increases the cultivation of water-intensive crops—such as rice, sugarcane, and cotton—that are ultimately unsuited to these regions (Damania et al. 2017). As a result, crop productivity suffers disproportionately in times of dry shocks due to extraordinary water needs that cannot be met. This increases vulnerability to drought, which magnifies the impacts of dry shocks.[12] *Ebb and Flow: Volume 2* (Borgomeo, et al. 2021) finds similar cases of maladaptive reactions to irrigation in the Middle East. Can this increasing vulnerability alter the economic incentives to migrate? New empirical results show that when irrigation leads to a dependence on water-intensive crops in arid areas, access to irrigation *amplifies* out-migration in response to repeated dry shocks, which is antithetical to the buffering effect seen in the overall findings in figure 2.3.

Similar patterns are also seen in cases in which irrigation becomes more uncertain and unreliable. When groundwater irrigation became less available or more expensive because of a declining water table in the Indian state of Gujarat, well-off farmers migrated to cities instead of seeking alternative adaptation strategies such as shifts in cropping patterns or more efficient irrigation technologies (Fishman, Jain, and Kishore 2017). With climate change and rising demands for water, irrigation water might become even more unreliable and scarce in the long run. If irrigation is not managed properly, its availability could also disappear quickly, for example through groundwater depletion. This would limit the use of irrigation as a buffer for agricultural incomes against erratic rains (Zaveri et al. 2016; Fishman 2018; Sayre and Taraz 2019), but with hitherto uncertain effects on migration decisions.

How Green Is My Valley: The Role of Green Infrastructure

An alternative but less recognized option to built infrastructure is the use of natural capital to bolster water supply and storage. Nature-based solutions draw on features of nature to enhance the ability of ecosystems and the natural environment to store more water, enhance water quality, and provide other critical benefits (Browder et al. 2019). Across local watersheds and even thousands of miles away, forests can alter the movement and availability of water by regulating flow, absorbing water when it is plentiful, and releasing it when it is scarce (Miller, Mansourian, and Wildburger 2020). Forests can also buffer the adverse effects of rainfall deficits on quality of drinking water supplies (Mapulanga and Naito 2019). Although forests—especially fast-growing plantations—may themselves use water and therefore reduce freshwater availability, there is growing evidence that, with proper management, forests can help enhance the resilience and quality of water supplies (Herrera et al. 2017; Mapulanga and Naito 2019; Miller, Mansourian, and Wildburger 2020).

In addition to providing essential environmental and water services, forests also contribute directly to the local livelihoods of millions of people worldwide (Hallegatte et al. 2015). More than 1.6 billion people live within 5 kilometers of a forest (Miller, Mansourian, and Wildburger 2020). This population often relies directly on the goods and ecosystem services that forests and trees provide (Miller, Mansourian, and Wildburger 2020). For many communities in tropical countries, forest- and environment-derived income accounts for as much as 20–25 percent of household income—a proportion that is even higher than that obtained from agriculture (Angelsen et al. 2014; Damania, Joshi, and Russ 2020).

Importantly, incomes from forests are less sensitive to weather fluctuations and droughts than those that depend on annual crop cycles because forestry relies on biomass that has accumulated over years or even decades (Noack, Riekhof, and Di Falco 2019). For this reason, the welfare-supporting role of forests is often greater in the presence of droughts, and households often end up consuming more environmental and forest goods than they would have without the negative rainfall shock to meet basic needs (Noack, Riekhof, and Di Falco 2019; Damania, Joshi, and Russ 2020).

This risk-mitigating role of forests and trees is especially relevant to rural poor people because they often lack access to other coping responses or other forms of insurance and credit markets to smooth consumption (Banerjee and Duflo 2010). Given the benefits of forests and the risks posed by water shocks, access to a forest's natural capital can alter the opportunity cost of migration.

Figure 2.3 shows the extent to which differing levels of forest coverage moderate water-induced out-migration (box 2.3). Results show that having greater access to forested areas reduces the impact of water shocks on net out-migration rates. In figure 2.3, the green bar captures the amount of reduction in out-migration that occurs in highly forested areas compared with the levels observed in areas with negligible forest cover (presented by the orange bar). The net effect is such that the buffering effect provided by forests lowers out-migration rates by about half relative to rates observed in areas with negligible forest cover. Stated differently, the loss of natural capital and the ensuing strain on livelihoods almost doubles the impact of droughts on out-migration. This suggests that forests act as a form of natural insurance or safety net in times of crises, and the income-stabilizing role of forests can have a considerable influence on the incentives to migrate.

Forests have a long history of providing means to mitigate and adapt to environmental change and drought (Hecht et al. 2015). In Niger, for example, afforestation was shown to reduce vulnerability to drought. During the 2005 droughts in southern Niger, mass migration and livestock losses, which had occurred during previous droughts, were avoided thanks to the buffering effect of the forests (Sendzimir, Reij, and Magnuszewski 2011). Depleting this source of income can therefore eat away at this important safety net and natural capital, reducing resilience to future rainfall shocks.

Unfortunately, such responses, as well as the general overextraction and overuse of ecosystem resources, can also lead to increasing degradation of ecosystems, which can undermine the sustainability of such adaptation strategies (Hallegatte et al. 2015) (box 2.4). Therefore, it is essential to

BOX 2.4: Water Shocks and Declining Wetlands

The rivers, lakes, floodplains, and deltas of Africa are rich, diverse, and productive ecosystems. These wetlands remain a lifeline and a crucial insurance against weather extremes. In the Sahel alone millions of people depend on the vitality of these wetlands (Madgwick et al. 2017). During the dry season, these natural assets are particularly sought after by pastoralists and serve as buffers against drought for large swathes of the region (Madgwick et al. 2017). But the wetlands are degrading and declining.

For example, the once extensive Lorian swamp fed by the Ewaso Nyiro River in Kenya has historically provided sustenance for pastoralists from far and wide in the dry season. Over time, it has been desiccated by diversions of water upstream for intensive horticulture, combined with overabstraction of groundwater beneath the swamp (Madgwick et al. 2017). Such wetlands can no longer serve as sources of refuge in hard times and have instead become sources of out-migration. In some places the pressure on wetlands is so severe that it has increased competition over access to scarce water and land resources, leading to increased conflicts and violent clashes (Madgwick et al. 2017).

Given the significance of wetlands for livelihoods and agriculture, it is becoming increasingly important to embrace agricultural practices that promote productivity while maintaining and enhancing wetlands and their ecosystem services. When trade-offs between agricultural production and the ecosystem services of wetlands are not managed, the conversion of wetlands to large-scale farming can lead to conflicts as pastoralists and small farming communities see their sources of livelihoods undermined (Bergius et al. 2020). As shown by recent Global Environment Facility and World Bank experience in Gabon, sustainable land management offers an approach to address competing uses of wetlands.[a] This includes improving knowledge of wetlands and capacity to monitor their status, recognizing and valuing the ecosystem services provided by wetlands, and making those services available to people vulnerable to shocks.

a. "Preserving the Vital Biodiversity of Gabon's Wetlands," World Bank, January 19, 2017, https://www .worldbank.org/en/news/feature/2017/01/19/preserving-the-vital-biodiversity-of-gabons-wetlands.

effectively manage these natural resources using tools that incentivize conservation without compromising the natural insurance properties of forests (Noack, Riekhof, and Di Falco 2019).[13]

IRRIGATION COSTS AND FOREST LOSS

The previous sections showed that access to the natural commons can influence water-induced migration outcomes. In areas where the forest cover declines, out-migration rates in response to rainfall deficits increase. What does it take to compensate for the drought-buffering effects of this lost natural capital? Can built infrastructure offset the effects of lost natural capital and, if so, how much would it cost?

Answering these questions is not easy. It entails an integrated portfolio of environmental management solutions to restore and protect natural capital while equipping farmers with productivity-enhancing irrigation infrastructure that buffers them against drought. Comparing information on forest loss with the cost of irrigation expansion is one way to try to answer this question and pinpoint the cost of recovering the buffering effect of natural capital lost due to deforestation (see box 2.5).

BOX 2.5: Irrigation Costs and Forest Loss

To assess the differential impacts of migration in places with low and high access to irrigation and forests, the analysis follows a similar methodology as described in box 2.3 and uses data on share of irrigated cropland at the start of the period over which migration occurs (Siebert et al. 2015) and data on forest cover from the European Space Agency. These data are used to construct time-invariant shares of irrigated cropland and shares of forest cover for the sample of grid cells. The analysis then adds two additional terms: interactions between rainfall shocks and shares of irrigated cropland and forest cover to the regression model. The coefficients on the interactions show the extent to which irrigation and forest access attenuate the migration response. These estimates are combined with summary measures of forest loss and irrigation costs. To quantify the cost of irrigation expansion, data from Inocencio et al. (2007) are used. These data are the most widely used estimates on the costs of irrigation expansion at the global level, and they provide unit costs of irrigation expansion per hectare by world region (for recent applications, see Rosegrant et al. 2017; Rozenberg and Fay 2019).

box continues next page

BOX 2.5: Irrigation Costs and Forest Loss continued

Case Study: Irrigation Costs and Forest Loss in Malawi

Forests make a substantial contribution to the livelihoods and the economy in Malawi, accounting for 4 percent of Malawi's total wealth and 7.5 percent of its natural capital in 2018 (Lange, Wodon, and Carey 2018). They contribute to livelihoods, jobs, and the economy through the supply of biomass fuels, sources of soil fertility, prevention of land degradation, and protection of watersheds (World Bank 2019). However, Malawi's forests now face a cycle of decline and degradation: between 1972 and 1992, more than half of Malawi's natural forests were lost. This loss amounted to an average annual loss of 2.5 percent (World Bank 2019). Since 1992, deforestation has continued, though at a somewhat slower rate according to the data set used in this study. Deforestation is associated with continued demand for agricultural land, charcoal and wood fuel extraction, and unsustainable timber production.

As a result of deforestation, important ecosystem services and the livelihoods they sustain have been lost. Forests no longer help buffer the effects of drought, whose occurrence is now associated with an increase in out-migration from areas that experienced deforestation. In Malawi, between 1992 and 2000, the ratio of forest area decreased by 13.7 percentage points, and at the same time out-migration increased by 12.57 percentage points in the areas that experienced forest loss.

Irrigation is one way to build resilience against drought and buffer its impacts on livelihoods. In the case of Malawi, estimates from the analysis suggest that 96,000 hectares of land would need to be placed under irrigation to compensate for the drought-buffering effects of the lost forest. At a unit cost of irrigation expansion (that is, without operation and maintenance) of US$16,226 per hectare (Inocencio et al. 2007), this would mean an investment cost of about US$1.563 billion. To get a sense of the magnitude, these cost estimates are similar to the levels of investment in Malawi's recently launched Irrigation Master Plan. The strategy explicitly considers the country's irrigation potential and suggests that US$2.146 billion for initial infrastructure and US$278 million annual recurrent costs would be needed to develop 116,000 hectares in the next 20 years (SMEC 2015). This suggests that the costs of recovering the buffering effect of natural capital lost due to deforestation are not trivial compared with maintaining and protecting forests.

This strategy will result in only an approximation because it ignores the costs and benefits of other environmental management solutions, and because the costs and benefits of irrigation expansion vary widely across the world. Nevertheless, it still does provide broad insights into the relative costs of policy options available to mitigate drought risks in areas with depleted natural capital.

The calculations are performed using the empirical estimation described in box 2.5 in combination with summary measures of forest loss and irrigation costs. Globally, on average, for a 10 percentage point decrease in the share of forest cover,[14] around 195 million hectares of land would need to be placed under irrigation to compensate for the drought-buffering effects of lost forest. At a unit cost of irrigation expansion ranging from US$4,000 to US$16,000 per hectare (Inocencio et al. 2007), this would mean an investment cost of about US$0.8 trillion to US$3 trillion.

These estimates show that the drought-buffering effects of forests are not trivial and highlight the underappreciated benefits of investing in forests and nature. Healthy ecosystems underpin economies and society on many levels. They provide essential livelihoods and environmental services, regulate key aspects of the global carbon cycle and climate, sustain cultural traditions, and offer health and recreation benefits. They also provide critical habitat for biodiversity. Although a comprehensive accounting of all of the benefits remains elusive, the costs of nature-based solutions are often found to be negligible and without large financial outlays or environmental damage, compared with other physical capital. Elsewhere, studies have shown that preserving floodplains from development can reduce flood damage by up to 78 percent, and using environmentally sensitive agricultural and land management practices can increase water flow by up to 11 percent (Watson et al. 2016; Abell et al. 2017). Importantly, natural capital investments can be complementary to infrastructure. Investing in a suite of solutions to buffer incomes from erratic rains—for example, protecting catchment areas and forests, together with a canal or dam for irrigation—can produce greater benefits than investing in any single one of these solutions (Guannel et al. 2016).

WATER AS A CONDUIT FOR DEVELOPMENT

Much of the study of development economics is concerned with why some places are poor and some are rich, which is closely related to why some places *became* rich and some *remained* poor. Underpinning this foundational question in development is the unfolding process of migration. It is the key channel through which standards of living can even out across regions such that people can take advantage of new opportunities and leave areas hit by economic adversity.

This chapter uses historical episodes of water shocks and their relation to migration to better understand water's role in shaping the issues related to this central theme within economics. It demonstrates that migration serves as a significant margin of adjustment in response to water shocks and persistent droughts. But it also highlights that this adjustment mechanism may not be available to everyone. Even as a closer study of economic incentives might predict movement in response to differences in economic opportunities caused by droughts, the real world is far from being "irrepressibly dynamic" (Banerjee and Duflo 2019). It is sticky and replete with friction.

The analysis suggests that for those with the ability to migrate, migration may have been instrumental in avoiding some of the grim outcomes of droughts and in building insurance against water risks. However, for the most vulnerable members of society, this option may not be available, suggesting that migration opportunities are only open to those who have sufficient social and economic capital. Supporting this argument, the study also confirms that for the poor, migration options are much more available in response to wet rainfall episodes that allow accumulation of capital and a greater adaptive capacity to migrate.

This raises an important policy issue. Those who experience reductions in employment opportunities or income because of drought, but who do not have the wherewithal to move, face a double dilemma. Not only are they the most vulnerable to the impact of water shocks on their livelihoods but also they are the least likely to secure their livelihoods through migration. These trapped populations are often hidden from media headlines, yet they represent a policy concern just as serious as migration that could have much wider consequences. The compounding of vulnerabilities could increase demands for humanitarian assistance, add to local stress, or even ignite conflict.

On the other hand, for those with the means to migrate, the fact that migration in response to dry shocks is substantial is also a reflection that other adaptation strategies, protective investments, and coping mechanisms are not readily available to all as a means of managing with less water and mitigating the impact of water scarcity on income. This chapter sheds light on these issues and shows that migration responses to water shocks can be attenuated in the presence of buffering investments in gray and green infrastructure. The income-smoothing benefits provided by irrigation infrastructure and forest access are able to diminish the risk of water shocks and in turn lessen the impact of water shocks on migration, even if they cannot eliminate the effect completely.[15]

But this is not true everywhere and at every time. If these buffering investments are not managed properly it may be that in the long run their benefits will also disappear quickly. When natural capital depletes with persistent declines in ecosystem services and irrigation becomes unreliable, they can no longer buffer income against droughts. There is also ever-growing evidence of irrigation giving rise to perverse incentives, which leads to moral hazard problems. The availability of irrigation in arid areas can create the illusion of abundance, which increases the cultivation of water-intensive crops that are ultimately unsuited to these regions. In these areas, irrigation can paradoxically accentuate the adverse impacts of droughts. The end result is increasing vulnerability that leads to even more distress migration.

This has important implications for long-term sustainability and growth. An optimal strategy would need to balance both short-run and long-run trade-offs. This would entail (a) improving rural productivity in the short run because it is often the case that the rural sector supports livelihoods for many and negative rural sector shocks driven by rainfall shocks can spill over to the rest of the economy (Emerick 2018); and (b) promoting resilience of communities in the long run, especially when fixed factor supplies of a resource such as water could limit growth. Ultimately, the costs and benefits of policies that enable people to move elsewhere need to be considered alongside any policies that encourage or constrain people to remain where they are (Foresight 2011). This is particularly critical in places where people may become trapped and increasingly vulnerable to high climate risks or where livelihood opportunities may shrink and become less sustainable in the longer term.

NOTES

1. There is growing recognition of this complexity in recent scholarship studying the migration–environment relationship (see reviews by Millock 2015; Wrathall et al. 2018; Hoffmann et al. 2020). These studies demonstrate considerable diversity in findings and reveal the contextually specific nature of the migration–environment relationship, which cannot be reduced to monolithic narratives.
2. Rainfall levels can have both positive and negative impacts depending on the context, which might weaken the average estimated effect. This is less of a concern for temperature because increases are more clearly linked with negative consequences (Hoffmann et al. 2020).
3. Grid cells that contain cropland areas that are higher than the 95th percentile of the country-specific cropland distribution.
4. These results are consistent with a collection of previous empirical findings that also find adverse temperature effects having a larger impact on migration in agriculture-dependent areas (Peri and Sasahara 2019; Hoffmann et al. 2020). Heat too can amplify the potential for migration across a range of water stresses by fueling the frequency of long dry spells, which in turn can increase the frequency of crop failure (Wrathall et al. 2018).
5. The risk that populations may remain trapped following weather shocks is consistent with previous empirical findings that have focused on the impacts of soil moisture deviations in West Africa (Flores, Milusheva, and Reichert 2021), various climate anomalies in Zambia (Nawrotzki and DeWaard 2018), repeated droughts in Thailand and Vietnam (Quiñones, Liebenehm, and Sharma 2021), and temperature increases on migration across the world (Cattaneo and Peri 2015; Benonnier, Millock, and Taraz 2019; Peri and Sasahara 2019),
6. Similar arguments for easing financial friction to facilitate migration have been made for Indonesia by Kleemans (2015) and Bazzi (2017) and for India by Munshi and Rosenzweig (2016).
7. Because the subsidy was delivered during the agricultural low season when productivity tends to be constrained and was targeted to areas thought to benefit from seasonal moves, the observed gains might reflect an upper bound on the returns to urban migration (Hamory et al. 2021).
8. Prior research has shown that, on average, large irrigation infrastructure provides a healthy boost to agricultural productivity. In most areas equipped for irrigation, agricultural yields show little sensitivity to rainfall variability (Zaveri, Russ, and Damania 2020).
9. Because wet shocks play a more muted role in driving migration outcomes, the results in this section focus on the interaction between irrigation and dry shocks.
10. Global studies that focus on international migration have also found that access to irrigation has the potential to modulate the climate–migration relationship in developing countries (Benonnier, Millock, and Taraz 2019).
11. For analytical purposes, these relationships are examined for the entire sample of grid cells across the baseline income spectrum to avoid sample size and power issues arising from slicing of the data into multiple samples and the inclusion of multiple interaction terms.

12. Other studies have documented a similar maladaptive reaction to irrigation in specific regions. One well-known study found that access to the Ogallala aquifer in the United States induced a shift to water-intensive crops that increased drought sensitivity over time (Hornbeck and Keskin 2014).
13. Migration in and of itself can also have important though complex and often ignored impacts on forests. In some countries, migration has allowed forests to recover or rebound as people leave rural areas and become less dependent on farming (Oldekop et al. 2018). In others, it has reduced forest cover as remittances allowed further expansion of cultivation (Gray and Bilsborrow 2014). The effects will vary depending on whether migration is one-way or "circular," how remittances are invested, and how migration interacts with forest management regimes (Hecht et al. 2015). Teasing out the various factors remains an important area of future work.
14. This is equivalent to the 95th percentile of the global forest loss distribution in the data.
15. Although the results in this chapter demonstrate two potential buffering strategies, other policies may also be equally as effective. Policies that reduce the exposure of a person's income to rainfall variability, such as social protection safety nets, weather-based crop insurance, or incentives to grow more weather-resilient crops, can also change a person's calculus when deciding how to respond to anomalies.

REFERENCES

Abell, R., N. Asquith, G. Boccaletti, L. Bremer, E. Chapin, A. Erickson-Quiroz, J. Higgins, J. Johnson, S. Kang, N. Karres, B. Lehner, R. McDonald, J. Raepple, D. Shemie, E. Simmons, A. Sridhar, K. Vigerstøl, A. Vogl, and S. Wood. 2017. *Beyond the Source: The Environmental, Economic and Community Benefits of Source Water Protection.* Arlington, VA: Nature Conservancy.

Angelsen, A., P. Jagger, R. Babigumira, B. Belcher, N. J. Hogarth, S. Bauch, J. Börner, C. Smith-Hall, and S. Wunder. 2014. "Environmental Income and Rural Livelihoods: A Global-Comparative Analysis." *World Development* 64 (Suppl. 1): S12–28.

Banerjee, A. V., and E. Duflo. 2010. "Giving Credit Where It Is Due." *Journal of Economic Perspectives* 24 (3): 61–80.

Banerjee, A. V., and E. Duflo. 2019. *Good Economics for Hard Times: Better Answers to Our Biggest Problems.* Penguin Books Limited.

Baseler, T. 2019. "Hidden Income and the Perceived Returns to Migration: Experimental Evidence from Kenya." Working Paper, University of Rochester.

Bazzi, S. 2017. "Wealth Heterogeneity and the Income Elasticity of Migration." *American Economic Journal: Applied Economics* 9 (2): 219–55.

Benonnier, T., K. Millock, and V. Taraz. 2019. "Climate Change, Migration, and Irrigation." PSE Working Papers halshs-02107098, HAL.

Bergius, M., T. A. Benjaminsen, F. Maganga, and H. Buhaug. 2020. "Green Economy, Degradation Narratives, and Land-Use Conflicts in Tanzania." *World Development* 129: 104850.

Blakeslee, D., R. Fishman, and V. Srinivasan. 2020. "Way Down in the Hole: Adaptation to Long-Term Water Loss in Rural India." *American Economic Review* 110 (1): 200–24.

Borjas, G. J. 1987. "Self-Selection and the Earnings of Immigrants." *American Economic Review* 77 (4): 531–53.

Borgomeo, Edoardo, Anders Jägerskog, Esha Zaveri, Jason Russ, Amjad Khan, and Richard Damania. 2021. *Ebb and Flow: Volume 2. Water in the Shadow of Conflict in the Middle East and North Africa.* Washington, DC: World Bank.

Browder, G., S. Ozment, I. Rehberger Bescos, T. Gartner, and G. M. Lange. 2019. *Integrating Green and Gray: Creating Next Generation Infrastructure.* Washington, DC: World Bank and World Resources Institute. https://openknowledge.worldbank.org/handle/10986/31430.

Brown, L. 2012. *World on the Edge: How to Prevent Environmental and Economic Collapse.* Abingdon, UK: Routledge.

Bryan, G., S. Chowdhury, and A. M. Mobarak. 2014. "Underinvestment in a Profitable Technology: The Case of Seasonal Migration in Bangladesh." *Econometrica* 82: 1671–748.

Cattaneo, C., and G. Peri. 2015. *The Migration Response to Increasing Temperatures.* Cambridge, MA: National Bureau of Economic Research.

Cattaneo, C., M. Beine, C. J. Fröhlich, D. Kniveton, I. Martinez-Zarzoso, M. Mastrorillo, K. Millock, E. Piguet, and B. Schraven. 2019. "Human Migration in the Era of Climate Change." *Review of Environmental Economics and Policy* 13 (2): 189–206.

Chen, C. 2017. "Untitled Land, Occupational Choice, and Agricultural Productivity." *American Economic Journal: Macroeconomics* 9 (4): 91–121.

Cuthbert, M. O., T. Gleeson, S. C. Reynolds, M. R. Bennett, A. C. Newton, C. J. McCormack, and G. M. Ashley. 2017. "Modelling the Role of Groundwater Hydro-Refugia in East African Hominin Evolution and Dispersal." *Nature Communications* 8 (1): 1–11.

Damania, R., S. Desbureaux, M. Hyland, A. Islam, S. Moore, A.-S. Rodella, J. Russ, and E. Zaveri. 2017. *Uncharted Waters: The New Economics of Water Scarcity and Variability.* Washington, DC: World Bank.

Damania, R., S. Desbureaux, and E. Zaveri. 2020. "Does Rainfall Matter for Economic Growth? Evidence from Global Sub-national Data (1990–2014)." *Journal of Environmental Economics and Management* 102: 102335.

Damania, R., A. Joshi, and J. Russ. 2020. "India's Forests: Stepping Stone or Millstone for the Poor?" *World Development* 125: 104451.

de Janvry, A., K. Emerick, M. Gonzalez-Navarro, and E. Sadoulet. 2015. "Delinking Land Rights from Land Use: Certification and Migration in Mexico." *American Economic Review* 105 (10): 3125–49.

de Sherbinin, A., M. Levy, S. Adamo, K. MacManus, G. Yetman, V. Mara, L. Razafindrazay, B. Goodrich, T. Srebotnjak, C. Aichele, and L. Pistolesi. 2012. "Migration and Risk: Net Migration in Marginal Ecosystems and Hazardous Areas." *Environmental Research Letters* 7: 1–14.

de Sherbinin, A., M. Levy, S. Adamo, K. MacManus, G. Yetman, V. Mara, L. Razafindrazay, B. Goodrich, T. Srebotnjak, C. Aichele, and L. Pistolesi. 2015. *Global Estimated Net Migration Grids by Decade: 1970–2000.* Palisades, NY: NASA Socioeconomic Data and Applications Center (SEDAC).

de Sherbinin, A. 2020. "Climate Impacts as Drivers of Migration." *Migration Information Source*, October 23.

Dell, M., B. F. Jones, and B. O. Olken. 2014. "What Do We Learn from the Weather? The New Climate-Economy Literature." *Journal of Economic Literature* 52 (3): 740–98.

Emerick, K. 2018. "Agricultural Productivity and the Sectoral Reallocation of Labor in Rural India." *Journal of Development Economics* 135: 488–503.

Fishman, R. 2016. "More Uneven Distributions Overturn Benefits of Higher Precipitation for Crop Yields." *Environmental Research Letters* 11 (2): 024004.

Fishman, R., M. Jain, and A. Kishore. 2017. "When Water Runs Out: Scarcity, Adaptation, and Migration in Gujarat." International Growth Center Working Paper. IGC-ISI India Development Policy Conference 2013, New Delhi, India

Fishman, R. 2018. "Groundwater Depletion Limits the Scope for Adaptation to Increased Rainfall Variability in India. *Climatic Change* 147 (1): 195–209.

Flores, F. M., S. Milusheva, and A. R. Reichert. 2021. "Climate Anomalies and International Migration: A Disaggregated Analysis for West Africa." Policy Research Working Paper 9664, World Bank, Washington, DC.

Foresight. 2011. *Migration and Global Environmental Change Future Challenges and Opportunities.* London: The Government Office for Science.

Global Commission on Adaptation. 2019. *Adapt Now: A Global Call for Leadership on Climate Resilience.* Washington, DC: World Resources Institute. https://openknowledge.worldbank.org/handle/10986/32362 License: CC BY 4.0 International.

Gottlieb, C., and J. Grobovšek. 2019. "Communal Land and Agricultural Productivity." *Journal of Development Economics* 138: 135–52.

Grabrucker, K., and M. Grimm. 2020. "Is There a Rainbow after the Rain? How Do Agricultural Shocks Affect Non-farm Enterprises? Evidence from Thailand." *American Journal of Agricultural Economics.* doi:10.1111/ajae.12174.

Gray, C. L., and R. E. Bilsborrow. 2014. "Consequences of Out-Migration for Land Use in Rural Ecuador." *Land Use Policy* 36: 182–91.

Gray, C., and V. Mueller. 2012. "Natural Disasters and Population Mobility in Bangladesh." *Proceedings of the National Academy of Sciences* 109 (16): 6000–5.

Gray, C., and E. Wise. 2016. "Country-Specific Effects of Climate Variability on Human Migration." *Climatic Change* 135 (3–4): 1–14.

Guannel, G., K. Arkema, P. Ruggiero, and G. Vertues. 2016. "The Power of Three: Coral Reefs, Seagrasses and Mangroves Protect Coastal Regions and Increase Their Resilience." *PLoS One* 11 (7): e0158094.

Hallegatte, S., L. Bonzanigo, M. Bangalore, M. Fay, T. Kane, U. Narloch, J. Rozenberg, D. Treguer, and A. Vogt-Schilb. 2015. *Managing the Impacts of Climate Change on Poverty.* Washington, DC: World Bank.

Hammond, L., J. Bush, K. Savage, and P. Harvey. 2005. *The Effects of Food Aid on Household Migration Patterns and Implications for Emergency Food Assessments.* Rome: World Food Programme, Emergency Needs Assessment Branch.

Hamory, J., M. Kleemans, N. Y. Li, and E. Miguel. 2021. "Reevaluating Agricultural Productivity Gaps with Longitudinal Microdata." *Journal of the European Economic Association* 19 (3): 1522–55.

Hecht, S., A. L. Yang, B. S. Basnett, C. Padoch, and N. L. Peluso. 2015. *People in Motion, Forests in Transition: Trends in Migration, Urbanization, and Remittances and Their Effects on Tropical Forests.* Center for International Forestry Research Bogor, Indonesia.

Henderson, J. V., A. Storeygard, and U. Deichmann. 2017. "Has Climate Change Driven Urbanization in Africa?" *Journal of Development Economics* 124 (January): 60–82.

Herrera, D., A. Ellis, B. Fisher, C. D. Golden, K. Johnson, M. Mulligan, A. Pfaff, T. Treuer, and T. H. Ricketts. 2017. "Upstream Watershed Condition Predicts Rural Children's Health across 35 Developing Countries." *Nature Communications* 8: 811.

Hoffmann, R., A. Dimitrova, R. Muttarak, J. C. Cuaresma, and J. Peisker. 2020. "A Meta-analysis of Country-Level Studies on Environmental Change and Migration." *Nature Climate Change* 10 (10): 904–12.

Hornbeck, R., and P. Keskin. 2014. "The Historically Evolving Impact of the Ogallala Aquifer: Agricultural Adaptation to Groundwater and Drought." *American Economic Journal: Applied Economics* 6 (1): 190–219.

Ibáñez, A. M., J. Romero, and A. Velásquez. 2021. "Temperature Shocks, Labor Markets and Migratory Decisions in El Salvador." Working Paper.

Imbert, C., and J. Papp. 2020. "Costs and Benefits of Rural–Urban Migration: Evidence from India." *Journal of Development Economics* 146: 102473.

Inocencio, A., M. Kikuchi, M. Tonosaki, A. Maruyama, D. Merrey, H. Sally, and I. de Jong. 2007. *Cost of Performance of Irrigation Projects: A Comparison of Sub-Saharan Africa and Other Developing Regions.* Colombo, Sri Lanka: International Water Management Institute.

Jagnani, M., C. Barrett, Y. Liu, L. You. 2020. "Within-Season Producer Response to Warmer Temperatures: Defensive Investments by Kenya Farmers." *Economic Journal* 131 (633): 392–419.

Kleemans, M. 2015. "Migration Choice under Risk and Liquidity Constraints." Unpublished.

Lagakos, D. 2020. "Urban–Rural Gaps in the Developing World: Does Internal Migration Offer Opportunities?" *Journal of Economic Perspectives* 34 (3): 174–92.

Lange, G. M., Q. Wodon, and K. Carey, eds. 2018. *The Changing Wealth of Nations 2018: Building a Sustainable Future.* Washington, DC: World Bank.

Lesk, C., P. Rowhani, and N. Ramankutty. 2016. "Influence of Extreme Weather Disasters on Global Crop Production." *Nature* 529 (7584): 84–87.

Madgwick, F. J., R. Oakes, F. Pearce, and R. E. Tharme. 2017. *Water Shocks: Wetlands and Human Migration in the Sahel.* Wageningen, the Netherlands: Wetlands International.

Mapulanga, A. M., and H. Naito. 2019. "Effect of Deforestation on Access to Clean Drinking Water." *Proceedings of the National Academy of Sciences* 116 (17): 8249–54.

Matsuura, K., and C. J. Willmott. 2018. "Terrestrial Air Temperature and Precipitation: Monthly and Annual Time Series (1900–2017)." http://climate.geog.udel.edu/~climate/html_pages/download.html.

McAuliffe, M., and M. Ruhs. 2017. *World Migration Report 2018.* Geneva: International Organization for Migration.

Meze-Hausken, E. 2000. "Migration Caused by Climate Change: How Vulnerable Are People in Dryland Areas?" *Mitigation and Adaptation Strategies for Global Change* 5 (4): 379–406.

Miller, D., S. Mansourian, and C. Wildburger. 2020. *Forests, Trees and the Eradication of Poverty: Potential and Limitations. A Global Assessment Report.* IUFRO World Series No. 39, International Union of Forest Research Organizations, Vienna.

Millock, K. 2015. "Migration and Environment." *Annual Review of Resource Economics* 7 (1): 35–60.

Mueller, V., C. Gray, and D. Hopping. 2020. "Climate-Induced Migration and Unemployment in Middle-Income Africa." *Global Environmental Change: Human and Policy Dimensions* 65 (November): 102183.

Mueller, V., G. Sheriff, X. Dou, and C. Gray. 2020. "Temporary Migration and Climate Variation in Eastern Africa." *World Development* 126: 104704.

Munshi, K., and M. Rosenzweig. 2016. "Networks and Misallocation: Insurance, Migration, and the Rural–Urban Wage Gap." *American Economic Review* 106 (1): 46–98.

Narain, U., S. Margulis, and T. Essam. 2011. "Estimating Costs of Adaptation to Climate Change." *Climate Policy* 11 (3): 1001–19.

Nawrotzki, R.J., and J. DeWaard. 2018. "Putting Trapped Populations into Place: Climate Change and Inter-district Migration Flows in Zambia." *Regional Environmental Change* 18: 533–46.

Nawrotzki, R. J., F. Riosmena, L. M. Hunter, and D. M. Runfola. 2015. "Amplification or Suppression: Social Networks and the Climate Change–Migration Association in Rural Mexico." *Global Environmental Change* 35: 463–74.

Noack, F., M.-C. Riekhof, and S. Di Falco. 2019. "Droughts, Biodiversity, and Rural Incomes in the Tropics." *Journal of the Association of Environmental and Resource Economists* 6 (4): 823–52.

Oldekop, J. A., K. R. E. Sims, M. J. Whittingham, and A. Agrawal. 2018. "An Upside to Globalization: International Migration Drives Reforestation in Nepal." *Global Environmental Change.* 52: 66–74.

Peri, G., and A. Sasahara. 2019. *The Impact of Global Warming on Rural-Urban Migrations: Evidence from Global Big Data.* Cambridge, MA: National Bureau of Economic Research.

Pokhrel, Y., F. Felfelani, Y. Satoh, J. Boulange, P. Burek, A. Gädeke, D. Gerten, S. N. Gosling, M. Grillakis, L. Gudmundsson, N. Hanasaki, H. Kim, A. Koutroulis, J. Liu, L. Papadimitriou, J. Schewe, H. M. Schmied, T. Stacke, C.-E. Telteu, W. Thiery, T. Veldkamp, F. Zhao, and Y. Wada. 2021. "Global Terrestrial Water Storage and Drought Severity under Climate Change." *Nature Climate Change* 11: 226–33.

Quiñones, E. J., S. Liebenehm, and R. Sharma. 2021. "Left Home High and Dry—Reduced Migration in Response to Repeated Droughts in Thailand and Vietnam." *Population and Environment* 42 (4): 579–621.

Ramankutty, N., A. T. Evan, C. Monfreda, and J. A. Foley. 2008. "Farming the Planet: 1. Geographic Distribution of Global Agricultural Lands in the Year 2000." *Global Biogeochemical Cycles* 22 (1): GB1003.

Ricciardi, V., A. Wane, B. S. Sidhu, C. Godde, D. Solomon, E. McCullough, F. Diekmann, J. Porciello, M. Jain, N. Randall, and Z. Mehrabi. 2020. "A Scoping Review of Research Funding for Small-Scale Farmers in Water Scarce Regions." *Nature Sustainability* 3 (10): 836–44.

Rigaud, K. K., B. Jones, J. Bergmann, V. Clement, K. Ober, J. Schewe, S. Adamo, B. McCusker, S. Heuser, and A. Midgley. 2018. *Groundswell: Preparing for Internal Climate Migration.* Washington, DC: World Bank.

Rosegrant, M. W., T. B. Sulser, D. Mason-D'Croz, N. Cenacchi, A. Nin-Pratt, S. Dunston, T. Zhu, C. Ringler, K. D. Wiebe, S. Robinson, D. Willenbockel, H. Xie, H. Y. Kwon, T. Johnson, T. S. Thomas, F. Wimmer, R. Schaldach, G. C. Nelson, and B. Willaarts. 2017. *Quantitative Foresight Modeling to Inform the CGIAR Research Portfolio.* Washington, DC: International Food Policy Research Institute.

Roy, A. D. 1951. "Some Thoughts on the Distribution of Earnings." *Oxford Economic Papers* 3 (2): 135–46.

Rozenberg, J., and M. Fay, eds. 2019. *Beyond the Gap: How Countries Can Afford the Infrastructure They Need While Protecting the Planet*. Washington, DC: World Bank.

Sayre, S. S., and V. Taraz. 2019. "Groundwater Depletion in India: Social Losses from Costly Well Deepening." *Journal of Environmental Economics and Management* 93: 85–100.

Sendzimir, J., C. P. Reij, and P. Magnuszewski. 2011. "Rebuilding Resilience in the Sahel: Regreening in the Maradi and Zinder Regions of Niger." *Ecology and Society* 16 (3): 1.

Siebert, S., M. Kummu, M. Porkka, P. Döll, N. Ramankutty, and B. R. Scanlon. 2015. "A Global Data Set of the Extent of Irrigated Land from 1900 to 2005." *Hydrology and Earth System Sciences* 19 (3): 1521–45.

SMEC. 2015. *National Irrigation Master Plan and Investment Framework for the Republic of Malawi*. Lilongwe: Ministry of Agriculture, Irrigation and Water Development.

Verner, D., and E. Tebaldi. 2015. "Drought, Migration and Social Policies in Drylands of the Middle East and Latin America." Informally published.

Watson, K. B., T. Ricketts, G. Galford, S. Polasky, and J. O'Niel-Dunne. 2016. "Quantifying Flood Mitigation Services: The Economic Value of Otter Creek Wetlands and Floodplains to Middlebury, VT." *Ecological Economics* 130: 16–24.

World Bank. 2019. *Malawi Country Environmental Analysis*. Washington, DC: World Bank.

Wrathall, D. J., J. Hoek, A. Walters, and A. Devenish. 2018. "Water Stress and Human Migration: A Global, Georeferenced Review of Empirical Research." Land and Water Discussion Paper, Food and Agriculture Organization of the United Nations, Rome.

Yamagata, Y., and D. Murakami. 2015. "Global Dataset of Gridded Population and GDP Scenarios." Global Carbon Project, Center for Global Environmental Research, Tsukuba International Office, Japan.

Zaveri, E., D. S. Grogan, K. Fisher-Vanden, S. Frolking, R. B. Lammers, D. H. Wrenn, and R. E. Nicholas. 2016. "Invisible Water, Visible Impact: Groundwater Use and Indian Agriculture under Climate Change." *Environmental Research Letters* 11 (8): 084005.

Zaveri, E., J. Russ, and R. Damania. 2020. "Rainfall Anomalies Are a Significant Driver of Cropland Expansion." *Proceedings of the National Academy of Sciences of the United States of America* 117 (19): 10225–33.

Zaveri, E. D., D. H. Wrenn, and K. Fisher-Vanden. 2020. "The Impact of Water Access on Short-Term Migration in Rural India." *Australian Journal of Agricultural and Resource Economics* 64 (2): 505–32.

Zhu, L., and F. Garip. 2020. "About Time: How Combination and Sequence of Weather Events Shape Mexico–U.S. Migration Flows." PAA Conference Paper.

CHAPTER THREE

WATER, MIGRATION, AND HUMAN CAPITAL SPILLOVERS

"Keep, ancient lands, your storied pomp!" cries she
With silent lips. "Give me your tired, your poor,
Your huddled masses yearning to breathe free,
The wretched refuse of your teeming shore.
Send these, the homeless, tempest-tost to me, I lift my lamp
beside the golden door!"

— Emma Lazarus, "The New Colossus"

KEY HIGHLIGHTS

- Evidence suggests that water shocks influence not only the number of people who move, but also the skills they bring with them.

- Workers that leave regions because of dry shocks and droughts are lower-skilled than those that migrate otherwise, and have lower predicted earnings.

- These migrants and their families may still be better off because migration allows them to adapt to risks of water variability in the absence of other options.

- Policy response must ensure that migrants have access to the education and resources required to improve productivity, mobility, and integration across regions

INTRODUCTION: THE HUMAN CAPITAL CHANNEL

Water shocks have a large influence on the productivity of farms, firms, and families in the regions experiencing them. Floods can cause devastating damage to local infrastructure and assets, which are costly to rebuild. Droughts can be even more insidious, generating long-lasting losses to households and to gross domestic product (GDP) growth through their effects on local agricultural productivity, food security, and the health of workers. But it is not just the regions experiencing water shocks themselves that suffer. The impacts of water shocks on productivity are not localized and can spill over to other regions, especially across interconnected labor markets.

This chapter focuses on how the effects of adverse shocks spill over across regions through the movement of workers, and their combined human capital, across markets. It presents evidence that water shocks influence not only the number of people that move but also the skills that these workers carry with them. Through this channel, water availability can influence the productivity and welfare of regions that host migrants. Analysis of education levels of labor movements between multiple regions across the world shows that workers that move out of regions with lower rainfall and frequent dry shocks usually bring with them lower skills. This translates into lower earnings for these workers and thus may adversely affect productivity and inequality in the host communities. As such, adverse shocks such as droughts can have economic consequences beyond the regions that they affect immediately. Whereas the previous chapter described the nuances characterizing the relationship between rainfall shocks and the *number* of migrants, the analysis presented in this chapter documents how rainfall can also determine the *type* of migrants, as characterized by their education levels.

FROM TEMPORAL TO SPATIAL SPILLOVERS

It is well established that the human capital channel serves as an important pathway through which the productivity effects of water shocks materialize. Water availability in early life affects individuals' health and education outcomes later in life, and thus influences their earnings potential and their contribution to GDP as adults. The effects of water shocks on productivity can thus, surprisingly, persist over time (Maccini and Yang 2009; Hyland and Russ 2019). Equally surprising is that the human capital channel allows for the spillover of productivity impacts across space. This transmission of impacts to other regions arises through the human capital channel as well—rainfall patterns determine whether migration entails the movement of high-skill or low-skill workers. The evidence described in this chapter suggests that differences in rainfall across regions are associated with differences in the skill levels of migrants originating from those regions (figure 3.1 and box 3.1).

The results reported in this chapter speak to a large body of literature on spatial sorting of workers, which posits that human capital is central to the connection between migration and development (Combes, Duranton, and Gobillon 2008 Gennaioli et al. 2013; Young 2013;). Workers with differing skills and education levels move across regions to work in the sectors in which they can earn the highest return on their human capital. The most productive regions of an economy tend to host a high-skilled and well-educated workforce, offering this group higher earnings and better amenities (Gollin, Lagakos, and Waugh 2014; Bryan and Morten 2019). Of particular significance is how wealth and education levels influence the constraints and opportunities that determine migration opportunities faced by workers.

How can water influence the type of workers who migrate? As shown in chapter 2, rainfall shocks can influence the number of migrants originating from a given region. Climate in general, and water availability in particular, determine an individual's decision to stay or move because they influence

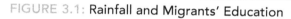

FIGURE 3.1: **Rainfall and Migrants' Education**

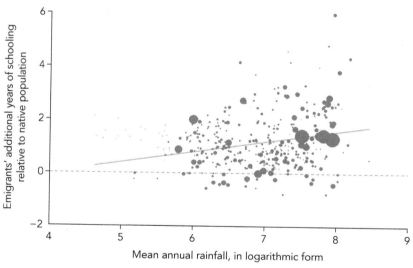

Source: World Bank figure based on analysis of demographic and economic data of 403 subnational regions covering 21 developing countries from Gennaioli et al. 2014 and climate data from Matsuura and Willmott 2018. *Note:* Figure 3.1 shows that (internal) migrants originating from regions with higher average rainfall levels tend to have more years of schooling compared with the natives of their place of origin. Each bubble represents a subnational region, and the vertical axis measures the difference between years of schooling of natives and emigrants originating from each region. The size of the bubble is proportional to the population of that region and only within-country migrants are considered in this analysis.

BOX 3.1: Examining Determinants of Migrants' Human Capital through Census Data

Chapter 3 examines how the education levels of migrants who move out of a region are determined by the water availability in their place of origin (determined by rainfall variation) by using statistical evidence derived from climate and census data for multiple regions across the globe. Because of the data required, countries included in the analysis are those that collect census data on individuals' migration status and their place of origin. These censuses usually record the migrant's previous province of residence, allowing for the climate experienced by the migrant in the home region to be measured. Statistical methods are then used to draw inferences from these data regarding how rainfall-induced water availability determines the skill-composition of migrant populations.

The first results presented in chapter 3 use such data for a large cross section of more than 400 regions from across the world, as described in box 3.2. The average rainfall experienced in the home region of migrants is positively related with the migrants' education levels, and regression analysis is used to confirm that this relationship is not driven by other confounding factors such as underlying economic and demographic conditions. But a well-known limitation of cross-sectional regressions is that they are prone to errors because observed relationships may be driven by unmeasured underlying variables. The second set of results, further described in box 3.3, dives into multiple rounds of census data from three specific countries to ensure that the cross-sectional results hold up to scrutiny when examined by more rigorous evaluation using panel-data econometric techniques. The availability of multiple census rounds at a decadal frequency for these countries allows for the examination of whether migrants moving in the aftermath of cumulative rainfall shocks have lower skill levels than typical urban migrants in these countries. The unpredictable nature of such rainfall shocks allows for statistical methods to credibly identify how *exogenous* variation in water availability can determine whether educated or uneducated workers migrate to other regions. Additional details of the statistical model employed are provided in the technical appendix to this report, available at www.worldbank.org/ebbflow.

the attractiveness of different regions and the wealth of rural households, especially through effects on agricultural productivity. The analysis of global data in this chapter reveals that higher rainfall is associated with migrants who are more educated than the native population at their origin (as presented in figure 3.1 and box 3.2). Workers that leave drier climates have lower levels of human capital investment relative to the native population than those workers leaving regions where rainfall is plenty. The next section digs deeper into this question by examining the relationship in three middle-income countries.

BOX 3.2: Rainfall, Education, and Regional Migration—Evidence from Cross-Sectional Data

Human capital differences, coupled with mobility restrictions, are a fundamental source of regional differences in development and productivity (Gennaioli et al. 2014; Tombe and Zhu 2019).

To further investigate how water can shape human capital and migration, data on internal migrants from more than 400 subnational regions from across 21 developing countries were analyzed, alongside demographic and economic characteristics of these regions, using socioeconomic data derived from Gennaioli et al. (2014). These data were merged with climate data from the Center for Climatic Research of the University of Delaware (Matsuura and Willmott 2018) to measure the average rainfall experienced by each region over the past 100 years. The regions covered in the sample are shown in map B3.2.1 and represent approximately 10 percent of the world's population. Most of the sample consists of middle-income countries, with only 52 of the regions found in low-income countries.

Analysis of these data suggests a strong positive correlation in the cross section between the average rainfall experienced and the difference in skill between natives and the emigrants leaving a region (see figure 3.1). The higher the rainfall, the more skilled the emigrants tend to be relative to the native population. The data suggest that an increase in rainfall equal to the interquartile range of this sample is associated with an additional half a year of schooling for a migrant leaving a region. This relationship is driven by regions in middle-income countries (where migration in response to rainfall shocks occurs, as found in chapter 2).

Weighted linear regressions were used for the econometric analysis of this relationship, using the population of a region as the weights (for details, see the technical appendix to this report, available at www.worldbank.org/ebbflow). The regression specifications control for other regional characteristics such as temperature, the size of the local population, urbanization rate, local gross domestic product, natives' education levels, and country fixed effects. Regressions are weighted by the size of the region to account for the precision of estimation using regional aggregates and to make them representative of the average migrant in the sample. Following suggestions by Solon, Haider, and Wooldridge (2015), the results are also confirmed to be robust to the use of alternative weights and simple regressions for estimation.

box continues next page

BOX 3.2: **Rainfall, Education, and Regional Migration—Evidence from Cross-Sectional Data** *continued*

MAP B3.2.1: **Regions Used in the Cross-Sectional Analysis**

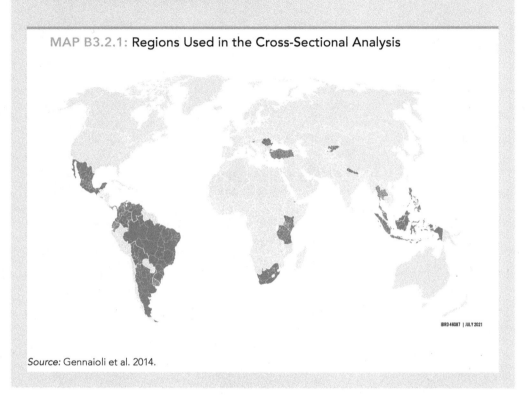

IBRD 46087 | JULY 2021

Source: Gennaioli et al. 2014.

WATER SHOCKS, DISTRESS MIGRATION, AND WORKERS' SKILLS

To gain further insight into the relationship between water, migration, and human capital, data on urban migrants from Brazil, Indonesia, and Mexico are examined (see box 3.3). These countries are chosen because multiple years of recent census data are available, with records of the place of origin of internal migrants and their education levels. This availability of data allows analysis of how water shocks from rainfall variation over time induced changes in the skills composition of migrants moving to urban areas. All three countries are defined as middle-income during the surveyed period, in which results from chapter 2 suggest that negative rainfall shocks would have increased internal migration of workers. New analysis in this section investigates the extent to

BOX 3.3: Drought and Rural–Urban Migration: Impacts of Cumulative Rainfall Shocks

Although the positive relationship between migrants' education and rainfall levels (as described in figure 3.1 and box 3.2) is robust to accounting for regional economic development and demographic patterns, there may still be unobservable characteristics, such as historical context and institutional heritage, that might confound such naïve estimates. There are many channels through which a positive correlation between rainfall patterns and migrants' human capital (as presented in figure 3.1) may be observed. Years of plentiful rainfall leading to income surpluses may allow households to save and invest more. Forward-looking families in regions with higher rainfall may choose to invest these savings in their children's education so as to allow them to move to regions with better employment opportunities as adults. Over time this could generate a positive relationship between rainfall and the education of migrants originating from that region. However, evidence gathered for this report suggests that dry shocks force the "distress migration" of lower-skilled workers who would not have moved otherwise in the near term.

To investigate this, data on urban migrants observed for multiple census years (1990, 2000, and 2010) for Brazil, Indonesia, and Mexico were analyzed alongside data on rainfall variation experienced in their region of origin when they moved (map B3.3.1). *It was found that migrants moving in response to frequent dry shocks were less likely to have attended high school.*

For each country the census data obtained from Minnesota Population Center's IPUMS International Version 7.3 was matched with climate data from Matsuura and Willmott (2018). The exogenous nature of weather variability over time was then exploited econometrically to draw causal inferences regarding the relationship between migrants' skill level and rainfall. Panel data econometric methods used to analyze these data suggest that migration in response to adverse rainfall shocks results in the movement of lower-skilled workers, irrespective of local development. Specifically, for all recent urban migrants observed in a census, the number of rainfall shocks experienced in their home region in the five years prior to migration was recorded. The analysis of these data alongside data on migrants' education levels suggests that migrants experiencing frequent dry shocks are less likely *to have attended high school*, when dry shocks are defined as rainfall 1 standard deviation below the long-run average experienced in the region. These results are robust to various econometric specifications that account for age, origin, destination, and survey year characteristics.

box continues next page

BOX 3.3: Drought and Rural–Urban Migration: Impacts of Cumulative Rainfall Shocks *continued*

MAP B3.3.1: The Subregions of Brazil, Indonesia, and Mexico Explored Using Census Data

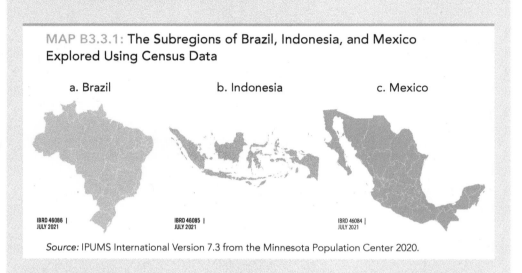

Source: IPUMS International Version 7.3 from the Minnesota Population Center 2020.

which the human capital of workers who are induced to move by negative rainfall shocks differs from that of other migrants.

Results from Brazil, Indonesia, and Mexico suggest that workers forced to move to cities in times of frequent negative rainfall shocks bring with them lower skills than the typical urban migrants in the region. The results suggest that each *additional* year of a dry shock experienced in the five years during which migration took place results, on average, in a 1.7 percentage point lower probability of the migrant being a high-skilled worker (in these cases, defined as having completed secondary schooling). Low rainfall in three out of five years in their place of origin reduces the likelihood of urban migrants being high skilled by 5.2 percentage points.

Successive dry shocks induce lower-skilled workers to migrate, but years of plentiful rainfall do not appear to have a consistent effect on the skills composition of migrants. Thus, it is the distress caused by negative shocks in particular that induces low-skilled migration. The phenomenon of migration in the absence of frequent negative shocks may simply be thought of as the sorting of individuals into locations where they are most productive and able to earn their best livelihoods. Workers who have accumulated more skills through investments in human capital tend to be more mobile and have more options. These workers are more competitive in the nonagricultural sector of the economy and tend to migrate in pursuit of higher earnings, even in times of plentiful rainfall. They move out of fertile high-rainfall regions into urban areas or manufacturing centers to earn greater returns on their human capital investments. Workers with lower skill levels stay in their home region in times of plenty, where they can earn agricultural incomes as farmers.

Rainfall variation directly affects farmers' incomes, and negative shocks can be particularly stressful for the least-wealthy households with poor access to infrastructure (such as irrigation), insurance (through credit markets and formal markets), or alternative income sources (such as a local manufacturing sector to work in). As shown in chapter 2, workers most vulnerable to the productivity impact of rainfall variation are likely to move in response to adverse climate shocks, provided they can bear the cost of moving. These workers also tend to have lower levels of human capital and their movement in response to adverse income shocks induced by climate conditions is associated with lower-skill migration. Additional evidence from India corroborates this, finding that climate migrants are selected from the lower end of the skill distribution and from households strongly dependent on agriculture (Sedova and Kalkuhl 2020)

In most cases, such workers will move to cities within their home country, where they are more likely to find nonagricultural employment opportunities, often working (and even living) in the informal sector. But such migration can also occur across borders. Evidence suggests that droughts in Mexico are associated with increased migration to locations in the United States where strong migrant networks exist. Nevertheless, more educated individuals are less likely to engage in such migration, possibly because they have better local diversification opportunities (Hunter, Murray, and Riosmena 2013).

PRODUCTIVITY, GROWTH, AND WELFARE

The implications of drought-induced migration for the productivity of cities and the larger economy are ostensibly different from other kinds of migration. Estimates from the data described in box 3.1 suggest that a reduction in rainfall from the 75th to the 25th percentile of this sample (that is, equivalent to the interquartile range) would imply 3.4 percent lower earnings for these migrants, reflecting lower productivity of the low-skilled migrants in the labor markets to which they move.[1] The lower productivity of migrants escaping dry conditions may have negative effects on the growth of per capita incomes in their host regions. City growth driven by such migration may not necessarily be conducive to further economic growth, and drought-induced migration may in fact be one of the factors leading to the phenomenon of urbanization without growth that has been documented by researchers (Fay and Opal 1999; Gollin, Jedwab, and Vollrath 2016). Evidence from Indonesia, for instance, shows that rainfall-induced internal migration tends to reduce employment and wages of low-skilled native workers in the host region (Kleemans and Magruder 2018).

Also, lower-skilled migrants are more likely to live in informal housing with poorer access to amenities (Niu, Sun, and Zheng 2021). Seasonal migrants often live in slums or are hosted by extended family networks. Their presence can be perceived by natives as adding stress on local amenities, public resources, and employment opportunities in their host regions, which in developing countries are often already struggling to provide for locals. In addition, the stress on local amenities may reduce property values in neighborhoods that house low-skilled immigrants, and such reduction can persist for decades as a result of the vicious cycle of low-skilled migration that is triggered because of the poorer amenities. For instance, evidence from Ambrus, Field, and Gonzalez (2020) suggests that the sorting of lower-skilled workers into cholera-affected neighborhoods in the aftermath of the 1854 Broad Street outbreak in London resulted in 15 percent lower property values 10 years later, and the differences persisted for up to 160 years to the present day. Perceptions of such impacts, although not necessarily always true, are often a source of animosity toward migrant populations (Card, Dustmann, and Preston 2012; Tabellini 2020).

Despite the potential adverse consequences for productivity and inequality in the host regions, it is difficult to make broader claims regarding how the migration of low-skilled workers induced by dry shocks affects broader welfare. At a macro level, mobility restrictions are a source of significant losses in overall national productivity (Tombe and Zhu 2019). In the absence of the choice to migrate, the families of such migrants may have been pushed below subsistence levels in their agricultural homes. The households sending migrants to cities in times of low rainfall rely on their remittances to pay for their needs in the absence of sufficient agricultural incomes (Lucas and Stark 1985; Black, Arnell, and Dercon 2011).

Arguably, the suffering averted in the home regions by the decision to migrate could be deemed worth the costs to productivity in the host region. For example, evidence from the experience during the Dust Bowl in the United States suggests that migrants escaping drought-hit regions had lower levels of education, but workers' ability to move out of rural areas limited the overall impact of the environmental collapse on the average wages of workers (Hornbeck 2020). In addition, evidence suggests that in the large cities a certain supply of unskilled workers is necessary to meet the labor demand created by the presence of the higher-skilled workers, for example to do jobs in the restaurant and construction industries within a city (Eeckhout, Pinheiro, and Schmidheiny 2014). Thus, the flow of skilled workers has the potential to be either a bane or a boon, depending on circumstances, and welfare claims are difficult to make without careful consideration of the context in question and its intricacies.

ADAPTATION STRATEGIES, ADJUSTMENT CHANNELS, AND REGIONAL SPECIFICITIES

In the absence of access to insurance and credit markets, migration may be an important coping strategy for households to buffer themselves against fluctuations in income induced by rainfall variability. The migration of low-skilled workers can be an important labor market adjustment mechanism, preventing agricultural wages of the poorest workers from falling too low. When few employment opportunities in agricultural areas exist, seasonal migration to urban areas provides an outlet for surplus labor during lean seasons. Longer-term emigration patterns observed in regions can be the result of the native population adapting to the risks inherent in agricultural economic activity due to climate or water variability.

Just as wealth generates differences in ownership of assets and in access to infrastructure that helps cope with weather variability, households' wealth also determines the ability to incur the costs of migration (Jayachandran 2006). The poorest households may be unable to employ migration as a coping strategy because of their inability to afford the costs and risks associated with migration, rendering them "trapped." Evidence suggests that easing fiscal constraints on the ability to incur migration costs by providing small loans or cash transfers causes households to send members to urban areas to cope with scarcity during the lean season (Bryan, Chowdhury, and Mobarak 2014).

Investments in education also determine the "profitability" of using migration as a coping mechanism, provided the direct costs of migration can be covered. Better-educated individuals are more likely to get jobs when they move to the city and thus can send back remittances to support the household members they leave behind. In fact, the prospects of skilled workers earning higher wages in urban areas may induce investments in schooling by households in the sending regions (Stark and Wang 2002). The migration of educated members, both seasonal and more permanent, allows rural families to diversify portfolios and reduce the risks of weather-induced fluctuations in household income. In line with this, evidence from Ethiopia suggests that households in areas with higher rainfall variability invest more in their children's education (Colmer 2019). In the face of a changing climate, investments in a portable asset such as human capital, which is not tied to a location, may be households' optimal approach to dealing with climate variability (Hallegatte et al. 2014).

Regional differences in the availability of opportunities outside of the agricultural sector can also be important. The availability of local manufacturing sector employment opportunities may allow an alternative in which farmers can work during dry seasons (Blakeslee, Fishman, and

Srinivasan 2020). If such opportunities are available, they may reduce out-migration of unskilled workers from these regions during times of stress. Consistent with this, the data suggest that the education of migrants and rainfall are not correlated for regions where large cities, and hence local nonagricultural employment opportunities, are present (figure 3.2).

FIGURE 3.2: **Migrant Skills and the Presence of Large Cities**

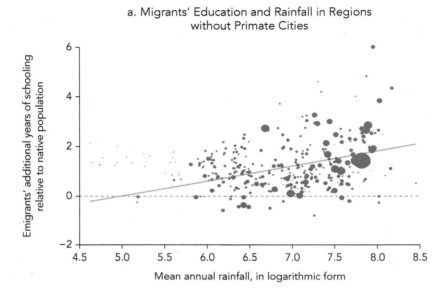

a. Migrants' Education and Rainfall in Regions without Primate Cities

b. Migrants' Education and Rainfall in Regions with Primate Cities

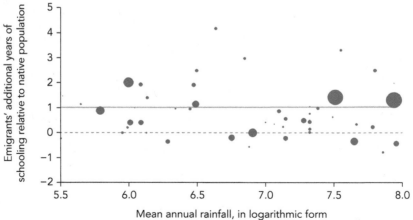

Source: World Bank figure based on analysis of demographic and economic data from Gennaioli et al. 2014 and climate data from Matsuura and Willmott 2018.
Note: This graph plots the same data as shown in figure 3.1, separately for the regions that contain primate cities (largest three cities of a country) and those that do not. The relationship between rainfall and migrants' skills is seen to exist in regions where large cities are not present because the presence of big urban areas is likely accompanied by local employment opportunities that discourage out-migration.

IMPLICATIONS FOR DEVELOPMENT POLICY

The presence of potential negative impacts of low-skilled migration on receiving regions and city growth suggests that the indirect social costs of negative rainfall shocks may be larger than the direct impacts. The spatial spillovers on the productivity of regions beyond those directly experiencing rainfall shocks may provide a rationale for channeling national resources toward investing in regional infrastructure projects, the restoration of natural capital, and social safety nets that buffer agricultural workers against weather variability. Particularly useful may be approaches such as adaptive safety nets or index-based insurance programs that can help build resilience to the effects of climate change. Mobarak and Rosenzweig (2013) find that the responsiveness of migration to rainfall is attenuated when workers are offered an index-based insurance contract. Similar arguments can be made to make the case for water storage capacity and nature-based solutions integrating green and gray infrastructure in agricultural areas to smooth the effects of temporal variability in rainfall. As shown in chapter 2, under certain conditions, such solutions can help build the resilience of farmers against weather variability and reduce incentives to migrate. By reducing distress migration, these solutions may also ensure that a sustainable form of urbanization takes place, one that is conducive to growth and leverages the sorting of workers into the regions where they can be most productive.

Nonetheless, migration is still an effective adaptation strategy for building long-term economic resilience to environmental change (Black, Arnell, and Dercon 2011; Hornbeck 2020). Existing evidence suggests that in some cases, providing agricultural households with the resources needed to migrate may provide much needed respite for financially constrained rural households. This may be a policy lever to consider in addition to other avenues such as provision of insurance and access to credit markets. It may be cost-effective to provide households with the cash transfers and microcredit loans needed to help them cover the costs of sending a migrant to urban areas in the lean season (Bryan, Chowdhury, and Mobarak 2014). But policy makers would need to evaluate this alongside the potential costs of inducing the movement of low-skilled workers to cities.

Moving to urban areas also allows workers to gain from the experience of living in urban areas. Workers experience growth in their wages after they have spent time living in cities, irrespective of their skill levels (Glaeser and Mare 2001; D'Costa and Overman 2014). And the "push" offered by water shocks might improve the wages of migrants and their families in the long run (Sarvimäki, Uusitalo, and Jäntti 2019). This suggests a strong argument in favor of the integration of low-skilled migrants into their host regions by removing barriers to mobility and ensuring access to basic services. To maintain public health, sufficient water supply and sanitation infrastructure must be in place in the dense settlements that are likely to host low-skilled migrants. Low-skilled migrants are also willing to pay for these basic services. In Brazil, migrant workers earning a minimum wage were found to be willing to pay R$390 per year to have access to better health services, R$84 for better access to sewage services, and R$42 for better access to electricity (Lall, Timmins, and Yu 2009).

More broadly, better accounting for the human capital dimension would allow policy makers to harness the power of migration toward the productive reallocation of labor for long-term growth. But caution is also warranted when considering policy responses. It may be tempting to consider, for instance, place-based policies as a promising tool for building national resilience if they provide an outlet for surplus labor during times of low rainfall or drought while keeping urban areas safe from the productivity impacts of low-skilled migration. But the costs and benefits of such policies need to be weighed carefully because investments in lagging regions must be sufficiently targeted to ensure that the expected benefits outweigh the high costs that can often arise from misallocation. Poorly targeted investments may disincentivize the productive migration of high-skilled workers into regions where they could make higher contributions to GDP. Thus, accounting for the interplay between migration and human capital is at the heart of the issue of ensuring efficient spatial allocation of labor across sectors in the face of climatic variability and increasing urbanization rates.

Perhaps the link between migration, climate adaptation, and human capital provides additional impetus to invest in the expansion of schooling infrastructure. If households are willing to invest in children's education to diversify their income portfolio in regions with high rainfall variability, it may be prudent to prioritize rural education investment in such areas. Such investments would ensure that if these children migrated as adults, they would carry competitive skills to the cities and regions they move to. Investing in human capital because of its portable nature would allow for higher returns for workers irrespective of whether they choose to stay in or leave their home region and can be a potent tool to *accelerate* the process of structural transformation (Porzio, Rossi, and Santangelo 2020). Policies aimed at investing in people rather than in places while increasing economic integration and mobility stand the best chance of incentivizing better allocation of human capital resources across regions.

NOTE

1. These estimates are based on returns of 8 percent per year of education, as found by Kraay (2019).

REFERENCES

Ambrus, A., E. Field, and R. Gonzalez. 2020. "Loss in the Time of Cholera: Long-Run Impact of a Disease Epidemic on the Urban Landscape." *American Economic Review* 110 (2): 475–525.

Black, R., N. Arnell, and S. Dercon. 2011. "Migration and Global Environmental Change: Review of Drivers of Migration." *Global Environmental Change* 21 (Suppl. 1): S1–S30.

Blakeslee, D., R. Fishman, and V. Srinivasan. 2020. "Way Down in the Hole: Adaptation to Long-Term Water Loss in Rural India." *American Economic Review* 110 (1): 200–24.

Bryan, G., S. Chowdhury, and A. M. Mobarak. 2014. "Underinvestment in a Profitable Technology: The Case of Seasonal Migration in Bangladesh." *Econometrica* 82 (5): 1671–748.

Bryan, G., and M. Morten. 2019. "The Aggregate Productivity Effects of Internal Migration: Evidence from Indonesia." *Journal of Political Economy* 127 (5): 2229–68.

Card, D., C. Dustmann, and I. Preston. 2012. "Immigration, Wages, and Compositional Amenities." *Journal of the European Economic Association* 10 (1): 78–119.

Colmer, J. 2019. "Rainfall Variability, Child Labor, and Human Capital Accumulation in Rural Ethiopia." *American Journal of Agricultural Economics*. doi:10.1111/ajae.12128.

Combes, P. P., G. Duranton, and L. Gobillon. 2008. "Spatial Wage Disparities: Sorting Matters!" *Journal of Urban Economics* 63 (2): 723–42.

D'Costa, S., and H. G. Overman. 2014. "The Urban Wage Growth Premium: Sorting or Learning?" *Regional Science and Urban Economics* 48: 168–79.

Eeckhout, J., R. Pinheiro, and K. Schmidheiny. 2014. "Spatial Sorting." *Journal of Political Economy* 122 (3): 554–620.

Fay, M., and C. Opal. 1999. *Urbanization without Growth: A Not-so-Uncommon Phenomenon*. Washington, DC: World Bank.

Gennaioli, N., R. La Porta, F. Lopez-de-Silanes, and A. Shleifer. 2013. "Human Capital and Regional Development." *Quarterly Journal of Economics* 128 (1): 105–64.

Gennaioli, N., R. La Porta, F. Lopez-de-Silanes, and A. Shleifer. 2014. "Growth in Regions." *Journal of Economic Growth* 19 (3): 259–309.

Glaeser, E. L., and D. C. Mare. 2001. "Cities and Skills." *Journal of Labor Economics* 19 (2): 316–42.

Gollin, D., R. Jedwab, and D. Vollrath. 2016. "Urbanization with and without Industrialization." *Journal of Economic Growth* 21 (1): 35–70.

Gollin, D., D. Lagakos, and W. E. Waugh. 2014. "The Agricultural Productivity Gap." *Quarterly Journal of Economics* 129 (2): 939–93.

Hallegatte, S., M. Bangalore, L. Bonzanigo, M. Fay, U. Narloch, J. Rozenberg, and A. Vogt-Schilb. 2014. *Climate Change and Poverty: An Analytical Framework*. Washington, DC: World Bank.

Hornbeck, R. 2020. *Dust Bowl Migrants: Environmental Refugees and Economic Adaptation*. Working Paper 27656. University of Chicago and National Bureau of Economic Research, Cambridge, MA.

Hunter, L. M., S. Murray, and F. Riosmena. 2013. "Rainfall Patterns and US Migration from Rural Mexico." *International Migration Review* 47 (4): 874–909.

Hyland, M., and J. Russ. 2019. "Water as Destiny: The Long-Term Impacts of Drought in Sub-Saharan Africa." *World Development* 115: 30–45.

Jayachandran, S. 2006. "Selling Labor Low: Wage Responses to Productivity Shocks in Developing Countries." *Journal of Political Economy* 114 (3): 538–75.

Kleemans, M., and J. Magruder. 2018. "Labour Market Responses to Immigration: Evidence from Internal Migration Driven by Weather Shocks." *The Economic Journal* 128 (613): 2032–65.

Kraay, A. 2019. "The World Bank Human Capital Index: A Guide." *World Bank Research Observer* 34 (1): 1–33.

Lall, S. V., C. Timmins, and S. Yu. 2009. *Connecting Lagging and Leading Regions: The Role of Labor Mobility.* Washington, DC: World Bank.

Lucas, R. E., and O. Stark. 1985. "Motivations to Remit: Evidence from Botswana." *Journal of Political Economy* 93 (5): 901–18.

Maccini, S., and D. Yang. 2009. "Under the Weather: Health, Schooling, and Economic Consequences of Early-Life Rainfall." *American Economic Review* 99 (3): 1006–26.

Matsuura, K., and C. J. Willmott. 2018. "Terrestrial Air Temperature and Precipitation: Monthly and Annual Time Series (1900–2017)."

Mobarak, A. M., and M. R. Rosenzweig. 2013. "Informal Risk Sharing, Index Insurance, and Risk Taking in Developing Countries." *American Economic Review* 103 (3): 375–80.

Minnesota Population Center. 2020. Integrated Public Use Microdata Series, International: Version 7.3 (dataset). Minneapolis: IPUMS. https://international.ipums.org/international/.

Niu, D., W. Sun, and S. Zheng. 2021. "The Role of Informal Housing in Lowering China's Urbanization Costs." *Regional Science and Urban Economics* 103638.

Porzio, T., F. Rossi, and G. Santangelo. 2020. "The Human Side of Structural Transformation." CEPR Discussion Paper No. DP15110.

Sarvimäki, M., R. Uusitalo, and M. Jäntti. 2019. "Habit Formation and the Misallocation of Labor: Evidence from Forced Migrations." Unpublished.

Sedova, B. and M. Kalkuhl. 2020. "Who are the climate migrants and where do they go? Evidence from rural India." *World Development* 129: 104848.

Solon, G., S. J. Haider, and J. M. Wooldridge. 2015. "What Are We Weighting For?" *Journal of Human Resources* 50 (2): 301–16.

Stark, O., and Y. Wang. 2002. "Inducing Human Capital Formation: Migration as a Substitute for Subsidies." *Journal of Public Economics* 86 (1): 29–46.

Tabellini, M. 2020. "Gifts of the Immigrants, Woes of the Natives: Lessons from the Age of Mass Migration." *Review of Economic Studies* 87 (1): 454–86.

Tombe, T., and X. Zhu. 2019. "Trade, Migration, and Productivity: A Quantitative Analysis of China." *American Economic Review* 109 (5): 1843–72.

Young, A. 2013. "Inequality, the Urban–Rural Gap, and Migration." *Quarterly Journal of Economics* 128 (4): 1727–85.

CHAPTER FOUR

THE COST OF DAY ZERO EVENTS

"We shape our buildings; thereafter, they shape us"

—Winston Churchill

KEY HIGHLIGHTS

- Day zero events, whereby water supplies in cities are weeks or days from running out, are becoming more frequent as migration-driven urbanization occurs at unprecedented rates and water supplies become more variable due to a changing climate.

- Although these events are concerning for many reasons, their economic impact was unknown—until now. This chapter presents new research that quantifies this impact and presents a discussion of solutions for reducing their propensity to occur.

- These events are found to be far more frequent than media reports have indicated, and the most extreme events can cost a city up to a 12 percentage point loss in gross domestic product.

- Although in some cases supply expansion through infrastructure (such as desalination plants) will be critical, truly solving this problem in the long term and in an efficient manner will require demand-side management. This will include both scarcity pricing of water and technological solutions that reduce water use within homes and businesses.

A HISTORICAL PERSPECTIVE ON DROUGHTS AND CITIES

For thousands of years, the Mayan civilization and other Mesoamerican societies dominated the landscape of the greater Yucatan peninsula in current-day Mexico and Central America. Great cities of over 100,000 residents sprang up along the coast and in the jungles of the peninsula, some of which remained inhabited for more than 2,000 continuous years (Sharer and Traxler 2006). Inside these cities complex societies arose, with written language, calendars based on celestial observations (Smiley 1960), and complex architecture that still stands after 1,500 years (Cobos and Winemiller 2001).

Around 900 CE, the archeological record shows the beginning of a dramatic change. Cities that had been growing in population suddenly started to shrink, while other cities, particularly those in the southern lowlands, became abandoned entirely (Douglas et al. 2015). The reason for the sudden collapse of these pre-Columbian Mesoamerican civilizations has been hotly debated by historians and archaeologists. Numerous explanations have been offered, including endemic warfare and overpopulation. Recently, a series of studies based on new paleoclimatic data have pointed to a new explanation—environmental degradation and drought (Bhattacharya et al. 2015; Douglas et al. 2015).

The city of Cantona, east of present-day Mexico City, is particularly interesting because of its rapid rise and fall. It is believed that migrants from the surrounding area started to move to Cantona because of increasing aridity, especially in the north (Evans 2008), causing the city to swell to about 90,000 inhabitants by 700 CE. That growth was short-lived, however, as the climate continued to change in the surrounding area, impacting the city itself. By 900 CE, internal unrest catalyzed by water and resource scarcity caused the population to collapse. By 1050 CE, fewer than 5,000 occupants remained (Bhattacharya et al. 2015).

LEARN FROM THE PAST OR BE DOOMED TO REPEAT IT

Could a modern-day city suffer a similar fate to Cantona? Such a fate is as unthinkable as it is unlikely. Nevertheless, the convergence of several headwinds is putting stress on global urban water supplies and threatening the sustainability of many of the world's great cities. Increased per capita demand for water is partially to blame, with urban demand for water in 2050 expected to be 80 percent higher than it is today (Flörke, Schneider, and McDonald 2018). In addition, alteration of the global hydrologic cycle due to climate change is leading to an increase in the number of extreme episodes, making water supplies less predictable. Perhaps most critically, unprecedented urbanization rates are causing cities to expand faster than water and other critical services can keep up, in many cases.

As shown in chapter 2, much (though certainly not all) of this urbanization is driven by water deficits in rural areas, driving former agricultural workers into cities in search of better opportunities. Cities have long attracted migrants for many different reasons; they tend to offer more services and amenities, new job opportunities and a chance to earn a higher wage, and protection against the vulnerabilities of rural life. In sum, economists have referred to this urban attraction as the lure of "bright lights." It is this lure that has allowed cities to become places of concentrated dynamism, where economic growth can compound and livelihoods can flourish. But there is a risk that these bright lights could begin to fade if urban areas cannot maintain adequate levels of services in the face of growing water resource constraints. Already, 30 percent of global urban residents live in areas classified as slums (World Bank 2018), where access to basic services such as piped water and safely managed sanitation is precarious at best. And even in urban areas, poorer residents, for example new migrants, are forced to live in areas that are more prone to natural hazards such as floods (Hallegatte et al. 2016).

Most studies concerning the water–migration–development nexus focus on the impacts of water shocks in rural areas and their influence on driving rural-to-urban migration. As the results in chapters 2 and 3 demonstrate, these are critical issues that are well worth examining. Nevertheless, it is often assumed that urban areas, due to their superior infrastructure, are immune to such impacts and that they can weather most droughts or extended water deficits with little cost. This chapter explores new research that digs deeper into the question of what happens when urban areas, which are typically the receiving regions for migrants, experience water deficits.

The last few years have seen several major cities approach "day zero," the day when water taps for citizens and businesses will be shut off because of a lack of water. In 2015, São Paulo, Brazil, a city of nearly 22 million people, came as close as 20 days to running out of water. This event came on the heels of an unprecedented drought, during which the Cantareira dam system, which is responsible for providing water to nearly 10 million residents, saw flows reduced by 75 percent for two years in a row (Kotzé 2018). Similarly, in 2018, three years of drought set Cape Town, South Africa, on the brink of reaching its own day zero. The date of April 12, 2018, was estimated as the day that the municipal water supply would fail. Water use was severely restricted and contingency plans were drawn up for residents to collect their daily water allocation from 200 points across the city (Alexander 2019).

One year later, Chennai, a growing southern Indian metropolis and home to 11 million people, was the next city to grab international attention for yet another day zero event. Three years of deficient monsoon rainfall had left three of the four main reservoirs of the city completely dry, with the fourth at less than 1 percent capacity. The Chennai event was particularly surprising because it was sandwiched between two extreme flooding events, one in December 2015 and another in summer 2019 that was the strongest in more than 25 years (NDTV 2019), thus exposing the fragility of a water system that relies primarily on a set of small reservoirs with limited storage capacity.[1] Still, difficult trade-offs exist in such highly urbanized areas, where new reservoirs cannot be built without displacing many people.

What these three events have in common is that in each case the city never actually reached day zero. Significant stopgap measures were put in place to fend off total reservoir depletion before renewed rainfall finally started to refill the reservoirs. In São Paulo, financial incentives were used to reward utility customers who reduced their water usage. These incentives were also coupled with water use restrictions, reductions of hydropower reserves, and the use of backup groundwater supplies (Ritter 2018). In Cape Town, efforts to ward off day zero included significant curtailment of water used in agriculture around the city, as well as significant restrictions placed on municipal water use, whereby residents were restricted to 50 liters per day (Arcanjo 2018; Booysen, Visser, and Burger 2019). In Chennai, water was sourced from the city's outskirts, often at the expense of uncompensated farming communities, and from tanker trucks that were deployed to carry millions of liters from faraway cities to stem the shortage (Varadhan 2019).

Despite the fact that day zero was not actually reached in these cities, large economic and social costs doubtlessly resulted. Water use restrictions place burdens on households by increasing the time and cost of household production, particularly for those of lower income who are less able to adopt low-water-use technologies (Renwick and Archibald 1998). Residents may turn to water from tankers, which can be of questionable water quality and lead to the spread of illnesses (Choudhury 2019). As in the case of Chennai, cities may even find themselves in competition with agricultural water users, which can inflame tensions and conflicts between the urban and agricultural sectors. It can also place significant burdens on businesses, which see their costs rise and productivity decline when water supply becomes less reliable (Islam and Hyland 2019). Finally, one may conjecture several other impacts. For instance, businesses, particularly those in water-intensive industries such as manufacturing, may be less willing to make investments in cities where water supplies are less reliable. Also, individuals may be less willing to migrate into cities if they expect that water supply issues will continue into the future.

Although day zero events in these three major cities grabbed international headlines, their water scarcity challenges are not unique (table 4.1). Indeed, according to the World Resources Institute's Aqueduct water risk indicator, 17 countries, which are home to 25 percent of the world's population, are under extremely high water stress.[2] Many cities in India only have municipal water available for a few hours a day. For instance, Shimla, a city in northern India, has outgrown its water supply and faces water supply shortages nearly every summer (Singh and Kandari 2012). Pockets of extreme water stress can manifest even in countries with relatively abundant resources. In the United States, between 2012 and 2016, California experienced an unprecedented drought, prompting the State Water Resources Control Board to impose mandatory water use reductions on more than 400 large urban water districts (Pérez-Urdiales and Baerenklau 2020). Drought reportage also tends to be far more common in large cities, despite the fact that medium-size and small cities tend to be highly vulnerable (Singh et al. 2021)

Determining the costs of these events is critical for planning solutions, particularly as their frequency and intensity are likely to increase, given unprecedented urbanization rates and climate change. In certain regions, a warming world could not only make such rare and extreme events become commonplace by the end of the century, but in a worst-case scenario could also make them 100 times more likely (Pascale et al. 2020). In addition, as global warming occurs, cities will warm faster than surrounding regions because of their design and density, leaving them at greater risk of heat stress and water scarcity (Zhao et al. 2021). This chapter, therefore, presents new research that attempts to quantify the economic impact of these day zero-like events on global cities at a macroeconomic level. To do so, it uses a new global data set that links urban water supply sources with cities, allowing identification of when cities are experiencing large water deficits.

THE IMPORTANCE OF WATER FOR GROWTH

Although no study has yet examined the impact of day zero events, there is a growing body of evidence that water scarcity can have significant and long-term economic impacts. By exploiting granular data on local water availability, this literature has documented both direct and indirect impacts of rainfall variability or water availability on socioeconomic outcomes. For instance, several studies utilizing high-resolution geospatial data on gross domestic product (GDP) with rainfall and runoff measures have shown that moderate to large deviations in water availability cause economic growth to decline (Damania, Desbureaux, and Zaveri 2020; Russ 2020). These studies suggest that such effects materialize through impacts on agricultural productivity and hydropower generation. Other studies that exploit survey data on workers and firms show that unreliable water supplies and water shortages adversely affect productivity by reducing workers' incomes, inducing lower sales for firms, and worsening health outcomes (Desbureaux and Rodella 2017; Islam and Hyland 2019).

These results are in contrast to a more extensive and slightly older literature on weather and economic growth that has often found significant impacts of temperature on growth, but not of rainfall (a review of this literature is available in Dell, Jones, and Olken 2014). These studies tended to examine impacts across large geographic regions, often using averages of temperature and rainfall at the country and annual scale. They therefore

Table 4.1: Drought Events in Major Urban Water Supply Systems

Event	Type of mitigation measures taken	Evidence of impact	Sources
Algiers, Algeria (2000–02), experienced its worst drought since at least the 15th century.	Water was delivered by tankers to the most affected areas. The city also increased reliance on groundwater by drilling 40 new wells, and implemented interbasin transfers by connecting the city's network to three dams located more than 100 kilometers to the west. Finally, several small-scale water desalination stations were constructed.	All of the dams supplying Algiers were in the "dead band," with critically low levels of water. In three successive years (2002–04), there were riots in front of state buildings in Algeria in response to water shortages.	FAO 2018, table 5 Ait-Aoudia and Berezowska-Azzag 2016, figure 3 Touchan et al. 2008 Kettab et al. 2004 Ward and Ruckstuhl 2017, p. 63 IATP 2002
Kunming, China (2009–11), suffered the worst drought in Yunnan province in many years that was exacerbated by the destruction of forest cover and a history of poor water management.	An interbasin transfer (Dianzhong Water Diversion Project) was implemented which cost ¥70 billion.	During the drought period 2009–11, 120 medium-size and small rivers did not have flowing water and 400 small reservoirs, dams, and ponds dried up. From January to June 2013, water resources were available for urban residents only at specific time slots. Hydropower generation dropped 50 percent.	Qiu 2010 Scally 2016 Wu et al. 2015 Jia and Anfei 2010
Quetta, Pakistan (1998–2000), experienced below-normal rains (triggered by a La Niña event) that resulted in a 30 percent reduction in rainfall over a two-year period.	Deep tube wells were installed to meet the immediate water requirements.	Surface reservoirs (Spin Karez) dried up completely. At least 1.2 million people in Balochistan were affected by drought, and more than 100 people died. There was an increased incidence of Crimean-Congo hemorrhagic fever.	Naz et al. 2020, table 3 Quetta District Government 2011 Khan, Selod, and Blankespoor 2019 New Humanitarian 2010
Istanbul, Turkey (2006–08), suffered its lowest rainfall in the past 50 years.	Phase I of the Melen Water Supply Project was accelerated; the project was due in 2009 but was completed in 2007 because of the drought.	Capacity of the city's water reservoirs declined to 25 percent.	Istanbul Water and Sewerage Administration 2012 Farooq 2018

table continues on next page

Table 4.1: Drought Events in Major Urban Water Supply Systems (Continued)

Event	Type of mitigation measures taken	Evidence of impact	Sources
Conakry, Guinea (2002–04), experienced the most severe drought in Guinea's recorded history.	There is no evidence of mitigation measures taken.	The two hydroelectric dams supplying the capitol with water nearly ran dry and hydropower generation was stalled. Most of the city's 2 million inhabitants went without electricity or water for six months.	New Humanitarian 2003 Bah, Diallo, and Morin 2007
Tegucigalpa, Honduras (1999–2001), recorded extremely dry Standard Precipitation Index values across the country, which signaled extensive dry conditions.	The city increased reliance on groundwater.	Water rationing (six hours per day only) was implemented and water tankers were brought in to supply water. The water utility saw significantly reduced revenues, impacting service provision.	UNESCO 2018 CEPAL 2002
Mombasa, Kenya (2005–06), a city with high vulnerability to drought, was hit by an extended period of drought.	The city increased reliance on groundwater.	Because women spent significantly more time looking for water, time allocation and productivity were affected. Food prices increased, which exacerbated food insecurity and malnutrition, especially among poor city residents.	Comte et al. 2016 Awuor, Orindi, and Ochieng Adwera 2008
Fortaleza, Brazil (1996–98), experienced its third driest year on record.	There is no evidence of mitigation measures taken.	Following the 1998 drought, there was a Dengue outbreak; research links droughts with higher potential for such outbreaks.	Pontes et al. 2000 Costa et al. 2016

suffer from the fact that water availability is highly localized. For instance, it is quite common that one part of a country can be undergoing a drought while another part has abundant water. An important lesson from this work is that it is critical to account for this localized nature of water availability when studying the impacts of water. Particular care needs to be taken when looking at cities because it is often the case that water is transported over great distances to supply a city. Thus, a drought far away from a city can have profound impacts, while a drought just outside of the city, or even within the city itself, may be benign.

QUANTIFYING THE COST OF DAY ZERO–LIKE EVENTS

Building on the lessons from prior studies, a new approach was developed to analyze the economic impact of day zero-like water scarcity events in cities. To do so, a global database was assembled that links urban areas with their specific water sources. This unique data set from the Nature Conservancy and McDonald (2016) links global cities with the locations from which they receive their municipal water supplies. It gives the location and name of water sources for more than 500 medium and large cities in the world.

The water points identified by the Nature Conservancy and McDonald (2016), and the cities they link to, are used to identify when cities are likely to be experiencing a water supply shock. This is done by overlaying a global database of historical weather from Matsuura and Willmott (2018) on top of the water points data. By looking into the past and examining what the typical rainfall is around these water points, it is possible to identify years in which rainfall is significantly below average. When several of these years are stacked together, it becomes likely that the water points are experiencing a prolonged drought, and the city is therefore facing a water shortage. Thus, the same "rainfall shocks" that are used in prior chapters can identify urban "water shocks," where cities are likely experiencing reduced water supplies. Details of how these water shortages are identified are explained in box 4.1. Finally, econometric analysis is used to estimate the impact of these shocks on city-level growth.

BOX 4.1: The Resilience of Urban Water Systems

Urban water systems around the world are designed to cope with droughts of varying frequency, lengths, and severity. It is neither practical nor affordable to design a system capable of providing water through any possible length of drought, so water supply systems are typically planned to meet a design standard, expressed as a return period (for example, maintain supplies without any restriction on use through a drought with a return period of 1 in 50 years) (Watts et al. 2012). There is no formula or standard engineering prescription to setting the "design" drought. The standard comes down to a typical risk-based trade-off between what the water utility or community in question is prepared to accept in terms of the frequency, severity, and duration of water use restrictions associated with drought and what they are prepared (or able) to pay to avoid these restrictions (Erlanger and Neal 2005).

Although the length of the "design" drought that urban water systems can handle varies depending on context, worldwide experiences show that long droughts lasting three or more years are typically more taxing for water supply systems. As shown in

box continues next page

BOX 4.1: The Resilience of Urban Water Systems *continued*

table 4.1, recent droughts in urban areas that resulted in major water use restrictions (such as cuts or countdowns) lasted three or more years. This is confirmed by Buurman, Mens, and Dahm (2017), who analyze impacts and responses in 10 cities that have faced drought since 2010, and show that most cities start imposing severe water use restrictions following two dry years.

Adopting this three-year period as a rule of thumb, the analysis calculates how much rainfall has deviated from long-run averages over each three-year period for each water point. This is done through the use of a z-score, which measures, in a particular year, the number of standard deviations rainfall deviates from the long-run average dating back to the year 1900 (for instance, a z-score of −2 standard deviations means that rainfall in that year is 2 standard deviations below the long-run average, which marks a year with a significant rainfall deficit that is only expected to occur two or three times every century). Summing these z-scores over three years allows a year of rainfall deficit to be canceled out if the following two years have significantly above-average rainfall. This is critical, as positive rainfall deviations, or wet water shocks, can replenish water storage facilities and mitigate urban water supply shocks. At the same time, if there are multiple years with significant rainfall deficits, these deficits will stack, and the calculation will record a very deep three-year water deficit for that city.

The Nature Conservancy and McDonald (2016) data set contains data on all water points for cities, and cities in the data set have anywhere between 1 and 28 water source points. Because the analysis is looking at rainfall, only surface water points (reservoirs, lakes, dams, rivers, and canals) are included in this study. Thus, cities that receive their water supplies strictly from groundwater sources or desalination plants are removed. The resulting sample is 171 cities in developing countries that have at least one surface water supply point. For cities that have multiple surface water supply points, the z-scores for each of the supply points are first averaged by year, and then the three-year sums are calculated.

Before proceeding, it is instructive to see how these water deficits are distributed around the world. Map 4.1 plots the locations of all cities in developing countries in the database. The size and color of the dots indicate the deepest water deficit that the city experienced from 1992–2013 (the time period of the study). Red dots indicate large and sustained rainfall deficits with a cumulative z-score of less than −6 standard deviations (SD). This means that rainfall deficits were, on average, at least 2 standard deviations below the long-run average in each year over the three-year period. This is quite a large and prolonged shock, which will undoubtedly put stresses on the city's water supply. And yet, at least six large cities have experienced such a shock between 1992 and 2013. Note that cities facing large deficits

MAP 4.1: Location of Cities Experiencing Deep Three-Plus Years of Water Deficits, 1992–2013

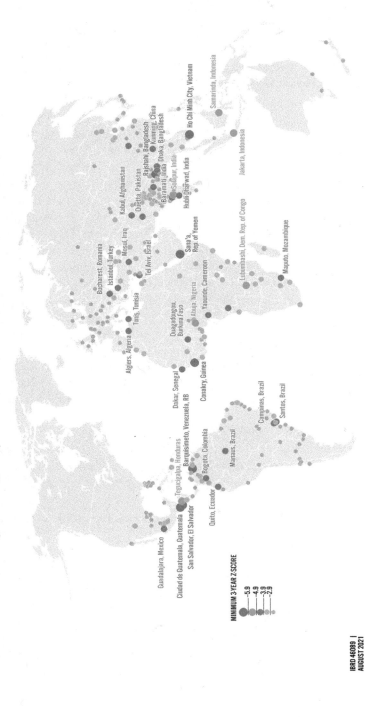

MINIMUM 3-YEAR Z-SCORE
-5.9
-4.9
-3.9
-2.9

IBRD 46089 |
AUGUST 2021

Source: World Bank map based on analysis using weather data from Matsuura and Willmott 2018 and data on urban water sources from The Nature Conservancy and McDonald 2016.

are relatively spread out throughout the developing world, though there are clusters of cities facing large droughts in South Asia, Central America, and northern South America. Notable omissions here are São Paulo, Cape Town, and Chennai because these droughts occurred after 2013, when the data set ends. Table 4.2 shows this in an alternative way, listing the full set of three-year periods when water deficits were greater than –4 SD.[3]

Table 4.2: Cities Facing Largest Three-Year Water Deficits

Period	Country	City	Water deficit magnitude (3-year z-score)	Period	Country	City	Water deficit magnitude (3-year z-score)
2003–05	Guinea	Conakry	–7.25	2004–06	Indonesia	Jakarta	–4.75
2002–04	Guinea	Conakry	–7.15	2002–04	Guatemala	Guatemala City	–4.72
2001–03	El Salvador	San Salvador	–6.62	2003–05	Cameroon	Yaoundé	–4.72
1995–97	Vietnam	Ho Chi Minh City	–6.52	1999–2001	Pakistan	Quetta	–4.68
2007–09	Yemen, Rep.	Sanaa	–6.43	1992–94	Indonesia	Samarinda	–4.65
2007–09	Venezuela, RB	Barquisimeto	–6.24	1995–97	Indonesia	Jakarta	–4.64
2001–03	Guatemala	Guatemala City	–6.15	1992–94	Brazil	Manaus	–4.61
2000–02	El Salvador	San Salvador	–5.93	1992–94	Bangladesh	Dhaka	–4.61
1994–96	Congo, Dem. Rep.	Lubumbashi	–5.90	1997–99	Indonesia	Jakarta	–4.51
1999–2001	El Salvador	San Salvador	–5.88	1997–99	Indonesia	Samarinda	–4.49
2004–06	Guinea	Conakry	–5.76	2008–10	Venezuela, RB	Barquisimeto	–4.47
1996–98	Indonesia	Jakarta	–5.64	2000–02	Burkina Faso	Ouagadougou	–4.33
1997–99	El Salvador	San Salvador	–5.63	1997–99	Guatemala	Guatemala City	–4.32
2008–10	Yemen, Rep.	Sanaa	–5.61	2006–08	Turkey	Istanbul	–4.31
1996–98	Indonesia	Samarinda	–5.54	1999–2001	Mexico	Guadalajara	–4.26
2009–11	Yemen, Rep.	Sanaa	–5.48	2008–10	Nigeria	Abuja	–4.25
2002–04	Indonesia	Jakarta	–5.45	2010–12	China	Kunming	–4.23
2009–11	Nigeria	Abuja	–5.32	1996–98	Vietnam	Ho Chi Minh City	–4.19
2002–04	El Salvador	San Salvador	–5.17	1997–99	Brazil	Campinas	–4.18
2005–07	Yemen, Rep.	Sanaa	–5.14	1992–94	Colombia	Bogota	–4.18
1999–2001	Honduras	Tegucigalpa	–5.13	1992–94	Romania	Bucharest	–4.16
2002–04	Indonesia	Solapur	–5.13	2002–04	Mozambique	Maputo	–4.15
1992–94	Bangladesh	Rajshahi	–5.09	1998–2000	El Salvador	San Salvador	–4.12
2003–05	Indonesia	Jakarta	–5.05	2001–03	Mozambique	Maputo	–4.11
2000–02	Honduras	Tegucigalpa	–4.96	2000–02	Algeria	Algiers	–4.09
2001–03	Indonesia	Solapur	–4.91	2007–09	Iraq	Mosul	–4.07
2006–08	Venezuela, RB	Barquisimeto	–4.88	1999–2001	Guatemala	Guatemala City	–4.04
2009–11	China	Kunming	–4.87	1993–95	Tunisia	Tunis	–4.03
2006–08	Yemen, Rep.	Sanaa	–4.86				

Source: World Bank calculations based on analysis using weather data from Matsuura and Willmott 2018, and data on urban water sources from The Nature Conservancy and McDonald 2016.

Comparing these water deficits against documented records of droughts shows that they correctly identify major droughts that occurred during the time period in question. For instance, the largest dry episode in the sample was for the city of Conakry, Guinea, from 2002 to 2005, which overlaps with the most severe drought in Guinea's recorded history (OCHA 2003); a very severe drought in Central America in 2001 impacted El Salvador, Guatemala, and Honduras (OCHA 2002); widespread droughts in Vietnam occurred in the late 1990s (Thilakarathne and Sridhar 2017); and the Republic of Yemen was significantly impacted by drought from 2007 to 2009 (Miyan 2015). The major urban droughts identified in table 4.1 overlap with this list, giving confidence that the methodology employed here is indeed identifying water deficits that resulted in significant urban impacts.

To measure the impact of these water deficits on year-over-year growth rates of urban GDP, a statistical technique for causal identification is used. Changes in the luminosity of nighttime lights, which have been consistently linked to changes in GDP at the subnational level (Henderson, Storeygard, and Weil 2012; Storeygard 2016), are used to measure changes in economic activity. Urban boundaries based on the presence of a contiguous built-up area (Khan, Selod, and Blankespoor 2019) are used to determine the geographic extent of cities, within which changes in nighttime lights are measured. More details are given in box 4.2.

BOX 4.2: Measuring the Impacts of Water Deficits on Economic Activity in Cities

The main empirical strategy for estimating the impact of water deficits on economic activity is predicated on the fact that rainfall and therefore water supply shocks are exogenous and consequently unpredictable with respect to urban growth. A statistical model is used to test how the growth of nighttime lights, a proxy for economic activity, changes in years following large water supply shocks. By controlling for other factors that may affect urban growth rates—like time invariant city characteristics, country characteristics, contemporaneous weather within the city, and time trends—the impact of the water supply shocks on urban growth can be isolated. And given the unpredictable nature, or exogeneity, of these water supply shocks, the results of estimating this statistical relationship can be considered to be causal—that is, if these shocks did not occur, the resulting changes in economic activity also would not occur. Specifically, the model uses ordinary least squares with the dependent variable being the annual percentage change in the growth of nighttime light luminosity, and independent variables that include an indicator for a water supply shock (which is the z-score of rainfall over the water supply points for the past three years); the annual percentage change in urban population; measures of contemporaneous weather in the urban area itself (precipitation and temperature); a measure of temperature in the water supply regions; country-specific time trends to account for country-level growth; year fixed effects; and urban area fixed effects. Additional details of the statistical model employed can be found in the technical appendix to this report, available at www.worldbank.org/ebbflow.

Results from examining the impact of these large water supply shocks are shown in figure 4.1. The figure shows the change in average city growth, as proxied by luminosity, which can be attributed to different water supply shocks of varying magnitude. Note that estimates of the impact of both wet and dry water shocks are included in the analysis. The impacts of wet water shocks, which presumably lead to additional water availability but could also lead to flooding under certain circumstances, are shown by the blue line. The estimated impact here is relatively flat with a statistically null impact. This is perhaps not surprising. If a wet water shock does not result in a flood, but merely results in the city having more water at its disposal, then it is unlikely that the city would see an economic boom from this because unexpectedly having additional water supplies available is not typically something cities can take advantage of. And if the wet water shock does result in flooding, there is strong evidence that shows that cities typically recover very quickly from floods. Kocornik-Mina et al. (2020), for instance, find that economic activity (proxied by changes in nighttime lights) fully recovers the year after floods occur, which is the time period examined here.

On the other hand, the impact of dry water supply shocks shows a monotonically declining impact on growth. As the magnitude of the three-year shock increases beyond a z-score of –3 SD, the impact becomes significant and large. Shocks greater than –4 SD, for instance, reduce the growth in luminosity by approximately 2 percentage points, and as the

FIGURE 4.1: **Impact of Water Supply Shocks on City Growth Rates**

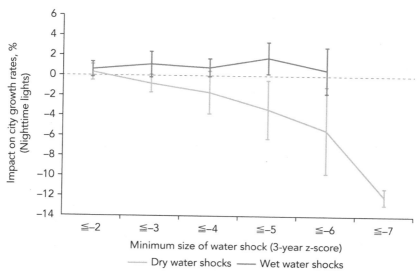

Source: World Bank figure based on analysis using weather data from Matsuura and Willmott 2018; Nighttime Lights Time Series Version 4, from NOAA National Centers for Environmental Information, Earth Observation Group; and data on urban water sources from The Nature Conservancy and McDonald 2016.
Note: Figure shows point estimates of the impact of increasingly large water shocks on urban economic activity with 95 percent confidence intervals.

shock grows to –6 and –7 SD, the impact grows to a loss of –5.5 and –12 percentage points, respectively.

How do changes in luminosity translate into impacts on economic activity? Henderson, Storeygard, and Weil (2012) have estimated that in developing countries the elasticity of nighttime lights to GDP is approximately 0.3. Others have estimated that this elasticity may be as high as 1 (Kocornik-Mina et al. 2020). This range implies that a shock the size of –4 SD reduces gross city product growth by 0.6–2 percentage points, and as the shock grows to –7 SD, the impact can grow as high as a loss of 3.6–12 percentage points. Compared with an average growth rate of 0.4 percent over the time period of the sample, this implies that even more moderate water supply shocks can send cities into deep recession.

Next, these results are expanded upon by looking at what types of cities are most sensitive to these water supply shocks. First, the cities in the database are split based on their long-run rainfall averages. One might conjecture that cities that are in more arid areas are more adapted to dry periods and have infrastructure in place that allows them to withstand these shocks. Indeed, that is what the results show. Figure 4.2 shows results from two separate samples. Panel a. shows the sample of cities that are in the bottom 50th percentile of long-run mean rainfall, and panel b. shows the sample of cities that are in the top 50th percentile. Although the cities in the top 50th percentile show a similar pattern to the main results, with large, dry water supply shocks significantly reducing growth, the cities in the bottom 50th percentile do not show as clear a pattern. It is only when the shocks become very large, or greater than –5 SD, that negative impacts appear.

Second, a similar exercise is undertaken but compares smaller versus larger cities. Again, the sample of cities is split into two based on urban population size. Results are shown in figure 4.3. Panel a. of figure 4.3 shows the impact of water supply shocks on the bottom 50th percentile of cities in terms of population, and panel b. shows the top 50th percentile. Here, it is seen that water supply shocks have greater impact on smaller cities, while impacts on larger cities are small and statistically insignificant. The greater resilience of larger cities to water supply shocks can be explained by several reasons. For example, it has been found that larger cities tend to use less water per capita than smaller cities. This is because water consumption tends to be tied most closely to the composition of economic activities within a city. Larger cities tend to be more service oriented and thus they tend to have shifted the more water-intensive economic activities to less populated regions. Smaller cities, on the other hand, are more likely to contain larger agricultural and manufacturing bases, which can be quite water consumptive (Michaels, Rauch, and Redding 2012 ; Mahjabin et al. 2018). Another explanation is that larger cities tend to have developed a more diversified economic base and are also more likely to serve as trade and migration hubs. This diversification enables them to be less vulnerable to idiosyncratic shocks such as water shocks (Gabaix 1999).

FIGURE 4.2: Impact of Water Supply Shocks on Urban Luminosity Growth Rate, by Climate

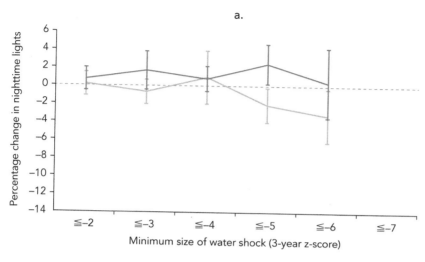

a.

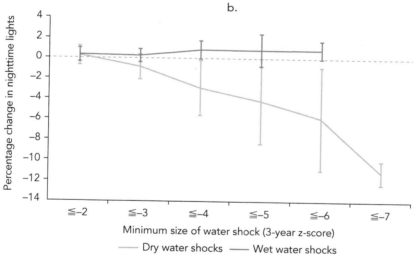

b.

─── Dry water shocks   ─── Wet water shocks

Source: World Bank figure based on analysis using weather data from Matsuura and Willmott 2018; Nighttime Lights Time Series Version 4, from NOAA National Centers for Environmental Information, Earth Observation Group; and data on urban water sources from The Nature Conservancy and McDonald 2016.
Note: Panel a. shows results for cities in the bottom 50th percentile of long-run mean rainfall, and panel b. shows results for cities in the top 50th percentile of long-run mean rainfall.

Finally, there may be a concern that the methodology employed here is misattributing the estimated impacts to water supply shocks, when in actuality some unobserved variable that is correlated with these water supply shocks is really to blame. To test the robustness of these results, it is therefore instructive to devise a placebo test—that is, a test with a similar setup, but one in which a similar result is not expected. As was noted in box 4.1, only

FIGURE 4.3: Impact of Water Supply Shocks on Urban Luminosity Growth Rate, by City Population Size

a.

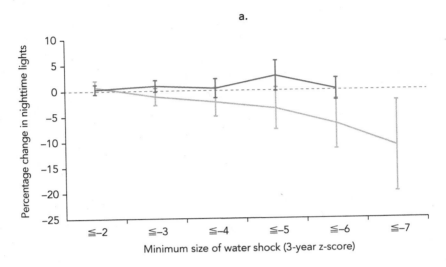

b.

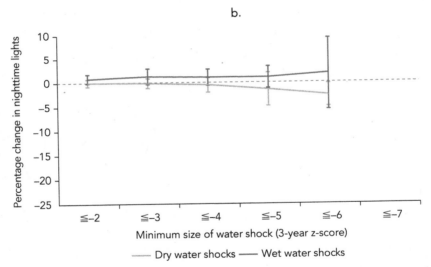

—— Dry water shocks —— Wet water shocks

Source: World Bank figure based on analysis using weather data from Matsuura and Willmott 2018; Nighttime Lights Time Series Version 4, from NOAA National Centers for Environmental Information, Earth Observation Group; and data on urban water sources from The Nature Conservancy and McDonald 2016.
Note: Panel a. shows results for cities in the bottom 50th percentile in terms of population size, and panel b. shows results for cities in the top 50th percentile in terms of population size.

cities that have water sources that include surface water were included in this analysis. This is because rainfall shocks are used to identify water shocks, and this link would not be as clear if the water source was groundwater[4] or desalination. Thus, there is an opportunity to look at cities whose water sources exclude all types of surface water, and test to see if rainfall shocks affect growth in similar ways. Results from this test are in figure 4.4. As the

FIGURE 4.4: Impact of Weather at Nonsurface Urban Water Points on Urban Luminosity Growth Rate, Placebo Test

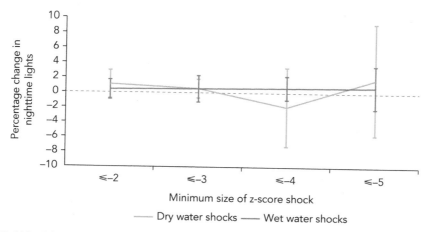

Source: World Bank figure based on analysis using weather data from Matsuura and Willmott 2018; Nighttime Lights Time Series Version 4, from NOAA National Centers for Environmental Information, Earth Observation Group; and data on urban water sources from The Nature Conservancy and McDonald 2016.
Note: Figure shows results of estimating the impact of weather at urban water supply points for cities that do not have surface water-based water supply points.

figure shows, the impact of both wet and dry shocks in these cities is a precise zero for all shock sizes. This result adds confidence that the methodology for identifying water supply shocks is appropriate and that the impact that is being identified is correctly attributed to urban water scarcity. It also suggests that groundwater and other sources of water supply, such as desalination and wastewater reuse, may have protective effects on cities.[5]

THE WAY FORWARD

The results in the prior section demonstrate the high costs that cities endure when faced with water supply shocks, and the critical importance of investing in policies and infrastructure that can enhance urban water resilience to ensure that cities remain the engines of economic growth that they have become. Urban migration and population expansion is very likely to continue into the distant future and cities must prepare for the realities of increased water variability due to climate change. Although a recession in a city is unlikely to reverse this process, it will inevitably slow it down, reducing the quality of life for residents and recent migrants alike. Still, adaptation to these events can also be expensive, and therefore it is critical that decision-makers carefully weigh the options available to them. These must include options that can expand and increase the resilience of water supplies, while also managing water demand.

Supplying Ever-Thirstier Cities

In the wake of a long and deep drought in the early to mid-2000s that threatened the water supply of Sydney, Australia, the government of New South Wales invested in a water desalination plant. At a cost of approximately US$1.4 billion to build, the plant was designed to produce up to 250 million liters per day, enough to supply 15 percent of the drinking water for Sydney's 2006 population, when acting at full capacity. Beyond the cost of construction, simply maintaining the plant on standby costs approximately US$150 million per year (Godfrey 2014), with costs increasing by approximately 50 percent to operate it at full capacity. Whether or not the construction of Sydney's desalination plant has paid off is an open question. The very year that the desalination plant went online, 2012, was also the year that the drought ended and the dams returned to 100 percent capacity. In 2019, the desalinated water production at the plant ramped up as Sydney's dams dipped below 60 percent capacity (Cockburn 2019). It remains to be seen how necessary the plant's water supply will be in the future.

Sydney is not unique in its decision to build a desalination plant after experiencing urban water shortages. In the wake of the 2019 day zero event, the city of Chennai made plans to build four new desalination plants to supply drinking water to the city. Similarly, Cape Town has also developed plans to construct a desalination plant as part of its water strategy for preventing future day zero events. Whether these expensive and irreversible investments will pay off is uncertain. What is certain is that desalination will not be a panacea for these crises.

Given the large upfront expenses of constructing desalination plants, and the fact that they are only feasible in geographies close to the sea, it is critical that decision-makers look both outward and inward to find alternative methods for increasing urban water resilience. Cities can look far beyond their boundaries and invest in natural infrastructure, which offers an often less costly alternative to built infrastructure. Across local watersheds and even thousands of miles away, forests alter the movement, quality, and availability of water by regulating flow, absorbing water when it is plentiful, and releasing it when it is scarce. As shown in chapter 2, the presence of forests can increase the resilience of rural areas to water supply shocks, and they can likewise have similar impacts on urban areas. Indeed, of the world's 105 largest cities, 33 rely heavily on nearby protected forest lands as a primary factor in drinking water availability and quality (Dudley and Stolton 2003).

Cities must also look inward to protect their water supplies and increase their water resilience. The resilience of a city's water supply can be strengthened by diversifying available water sources. Recycling wastewater and harvesting stormwater provide alternative sources to water supply while also providing a range of additional environmental benefits (Grant et al. 2012). "Blue" and "green" spaces in urban environments can also be expanded and revitalized to provide better flood protection and to capture water runoff, which can be purified and used for urban consumption. This model, known as the "sponge city" concept, is being developed in some cities in China (Chan et al. 2018). The plan exploits parklands, permeable pavements, and infrastructure (such as underground storage tanks) to soak up and store precipitation so that 70 percent of rainwater that falls on urban spaces is eventually reused. Initiatives such as these can partially reverse some of the harmful ecological impacts of cities while building resilience against rainfall variability and increasing the number of parklands and open areas for urban residents to enjoy.

Doing More with Less

As highlighted previously, expanding water supplies in many geographies can be risky, as well as prohibitively expensive. And in many geographies, particularly those that are inland, expanding water supplies can be infeasible. Therefore, the remaining options left to decision-makers are to limit urban growth in these regions, to reallocate water from other regions (typically agriculture), or to implement policies to reduce water use in urban areas.

In most geographies around the world, particularly in developing countries, the price of water is so low that it signals to users that water is abundant, even if it is not. This failure to incentivize efficient water use leads to perverse outcomes where there is nearly no link between water availability and water efficiency around the world. Figure 4.5 shows the relationship at a national level, comparing nonagricultural water intensity (x-axis)—that is, cubic meters of nonagricultural water withdrawals per unit of nonagricultural GDP—with water availability per capita (y-axis). By removing agricultural water use and agricultural value added from GDP, it is possible to get a sense of the dynamics in predominantly urban areas. If proper economic incentives were in place, one would expect a pattern in which countries line up along the 45-degree diagonal, with countries with less (more) water availability per capita having less (more) water-intensive urban areas. Instead, the figure shows little to no relationship between these indicators.

One important way to establish the economic link between water scarcity and its price is to reform subsidies in the sector. Few urban services are as subsidized as municipal water supplies. A recent World Bank study found that subsidies in the water supply and sanitation sector were as high as US$320 billion per year, as much as 2.4 percent of regional GDP, with urban expenditures accounting for 76 percent of this subsidy (Andres et al. 2019). These subsidies would be justifiable if they went predominantly toward low-income households to ensure access and availability to the most vulnerable. Unfortunately, the same study found that a mere 6 percent of water supply and sanitation subsidies were captured by the poorest 20 percent of the population, whereas 56 percent of subsidies accrued to the

FIGURE 4.5: **Comparison of Water-Intensive and Water-Scarce Economies, Nonagricultural**

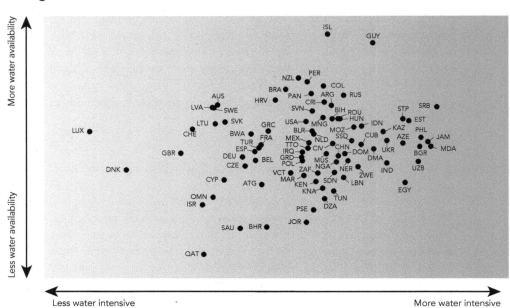

Source: World Bank figure based on water usage and scarcity data from AQUASTAT database of the Food and Agriculture Organization (FAO), and output data from World Bank Development Indicators. For a list of the 3-letter country codes used by the World Bank, please go to https://datahelpdesk.worldbank.org /knowledgebase/articles/906519-world -bank-country-and-lending-groups.

wealthiest 20 percent. Instead of ensuring access, these subsidies push the price of water so low that inefficiency is incentivized, service sustainability is threatened, and resources are overexploited. Subsidy reform in the water supply and sanitation sector is therefore critical for reducing the risk of future day zero events.

Another important tool for enabling decision-makers to respond to day zero events is dynamically efficient volumetric water pricing, which incorporates the scarcity price of water into the current price that is paid by households to minimize the average water tariff paid by households over time (Grafton, Chu, and Kompas 2015). One of the criticisms of the Sydney response to the day zero event is that the decision to build the desalination plant was made prematurely. The water regulations at the time were set up in a way in which the water utility, the Sydney Water Corporation, received a rate of return on every dollar spent on capital expenditures. Thus, the utility was incentivized to invest in expensive solutions such as the desalination plant, rather than promoting more sustainable use of water by raising the water tariff when water availability began to decline. Indeed, the utility had little choice because the regulatory framework at the time imposed prices that were based on the cost of service and not the scarcity of water. Thus, by adding a component of the price of water that is based on physical water scarcity, investment in capital-intensive infrastructure that augments water supplies (such as a desalination plant) could be delayed. In the long run, this can be important for both saving consumers' money and avoiding day zero events.

Technology and Behavioral Change

One of the major challenges with incentivizing lower use of water is that even when price incentives are put in place, behavioral change can be slow. This is true for several reasons. For one, as many studies have shown, the price elasticity of water is quite low (Espey, Espey, and Shaw 1997; Arbués, Garcia-Valiñas, and Martínez-Espiñeira 2003; Dalhuisen et al. 2003; Worthington and Hoffman 2008; Nauges and Whittington 2010). This means that changes in the price of water tend to lead to relatively small changes in the quantity of water demanded. This does not mean that pricing is futile, however, and there is some evidence that as the price of water rises, consumers begin to become more sensitive to changes in price. For instance, Rinaudo, Neverre, and Montginoul (2012) estimated that a 50 percent increase in the marginal price of water in southern France would generate 3 million cubic meters of water savings, enough to postpone water supply expansion in the study location by six years. And the simulations of Fuente (2017) for Nairobi suggest that there would be a 19 percent reduction in water use from transition to full cost recovery pricing over a 10-year period relative to business-as-usual pricing.

Another difficulty with using pricing to change behavior is that consumers typically have little information on how much water they are using, and which activities are using the most water. Without this information, it is difficult for households to make decisions about limiting water use. New "smart" meters offer a promising solution to this problem. These meters can monitor water use in real time, which allows households to visualize and predict their own water consumption (Demerle 2020). They can also measure water pressure and flow and therefore detect leaks, which account for losses of up to 60 percent of water supply in many cities (Moe and Rheingans 2006).

Other technological innovations will be critical for changing behavior and making cities more water resilient. One initiative leading the way in this effort is the 50 Liter Home Coalition spearheaded by Procter & Gamble and supported by the World Economic Forum, the 2030 Water Resources Group, and the World Business Council for Sustainable Development. The 50 Liter Home Coalition, which was born out of the Cape Town day zero event when households were restricted to 50 liters of water use per day, aims to demonstrate that not only is it feasible to live on 50 liters of water per day, but it can be done at little sacrifice to the household. The coalition is developing methods to treat water at the point of use to make it reusable. Thus, some wastewater can be treated to become drinkable, while other water can be treated for reuse (such as shower water repurposed for toilet reuse). Closing the loop on water use within the household can go a long way to solving water challenges and making cities more sustainable.

NOTES

1. Most recently in January 2021, droughts due to poor rainfall in Turkey have stressed the country's largest cities, including Istanbul, a city of 17 million people, and the capital Ankara. Istanbul was reportedly within 45 days of running out of water (McKernan 2021).
2. World Resources Institute water risk country rankings: https://www.wri.org /applications/aqueduct/country-rankings/.
3. Note that the earliest time period in the table is 1989–1991 because this indicator is lagged in the econometric model and thus would have its impact measured in 1992.
4. Although rainfall deviations would certainly affect groundwater supplies through aquifer recharge, this process is much slower and therefore one would expect to see a much more muted impact, if any, of groundwater sources.
5. Nevertheless, sustainability of groundwater resources is a critical concern that is outside the scope of this chapter.

REFERENCES

Ait-Aoudia, M. N., and E. Berezowska-Azzag. 2016. "Water Resources Carrying Capacity Assessment: The Case of Algeria's Capital City." *Habitat International* 58: 51–58.

Alexander, C. 2019. "Cape Town's 'Day Zero' Water Crisis, One Year Later." *Bloomberg CityLab*, April 12.

Andres, L. A., M. Thibert, C. Lombana Cordoba, A. V. Danilenko, G. Joseph, and C. Borja-Vega. 2019. *Doing More with Less: Smarter Subsidies for Water Supply and Sanitation.* Washington, DC: World Bank. https://openknowledge. worldbank.org/handle/10986/32277.

Arbués, F., M. A. Garcia-Valiñas, and R. Martínez-Espiñeira. 2003. "Estimation of Residential Water Demand: A State-of-the-Art Review." *Journal of Socio-Economics* 32 (1): 81–102.

Arcanjo, M. 2018. "Delaying Day Zero: Fighting Back against Water Insecurity." *Climate Institute*, April 16.

Awuor, C. B., V. A. Orindi, and A. Ochieng Adwera. 2008. "Climate Change and Coastal Cities: The Case of Mombasa, Kenya." *Environment and Urbanization* 20 (1): 231–42.

Bah, A. K., A. Diallo, and R. Morin. 2007. "Approvisionnement en eau des ménages de Conakry." *Afrique Contemporaine* 221 (1): 225–45.

Bhattacharya, T., R. Byrne, H. Böhnel, K. Wogau, U. Kienel, B. L. Ingram, and S. Zimmerman. 2015. "Cultural Implications of Late Holocene Climate Change in the Cuenca Oriental, Mexico." *Proceedings of the National Academy of Sciences* 112 (6): 1693–8.

Booysen, M. J., M. Visser, and R. Burger. 2019. "Temporal Case Study of Household Behavioural Response to Cape Town's 'Day Zero' Using Smart Meter Data." *Water Research* 149: 414–20.

Buurman, J., M. J. Mens, and R. J. Dahm. 2017. "Strategies for Urban Drought Risk Management: A Comparison of 10 Large Cities." *International Journal of Water Resources Development* 33 (1): 31–50.

CEPAL. 2002. El Impaco Socioeconomico y Ambiental De Al Sequia De 2001 En Centroamerica. https://www.gfdrr.org/sites/default/files/publication/pda -2001-centralamerica.pdf.

Chan, F. K., J. Griffiths, E. Higgitt, S. Xu, F. Zhu, Y. T. Tang, Y. Xu, and C. Thorne. 2018. "'Sponge City' in China: A Breakthrough of Planning and Flood Risk Management in the Urban Context." *Land Use Policy* 76: 772–78.

Choudhury, S. 2019. "Sewage Water in Tap: Chennai Water Crisis Throws Up Horror Stories." *India Today*, June 24.

Cobos, R., and T. L. Winemiller. 2001. "The Late and Terminal Classic-Period Causeway Systems of Chichen Itza, Yucatan, Mexico." *Ancient Mesoamerica* 12 (2): 283.

Cockburn, P. 2019. "Sydney's Desalination Plant Is Turned On: So What Does That Mean?" *ABC News*, January 27.

Comte, J. C., R. Cassidy, J. Obando, N. Robins, K. Ibrahim, S. Melchioly, I. Mjemah, H. Shauri, A. Bourhane, I. Mohamed, C. Noe, B. Mwega, M. Makokha, J. L. Join, O. Banton, and J. Davies. 2016. "Challenges in Groundwater Resource Management in Coastal Aquifers of East Africa: Investigations and Lessons Learnt in the Comoros Islands, Kenya and Tanzania." *Journal of Hydrology: Regional Studies* 5: 179–99.

Costa, D. D., T. A. da Silva Pereira, C. R. Fragoso Jr., K. Madani, and C. B. Uvo. 2016. "Understanding Drought Dynamics during Dry Season in Eastern Northeast Brazil." *Frontiers in Earth Science* 4: 69.

Dalhuisen, J. M., R. J. G. M. Florax, H. L. F. de Groot, and P. Nijkamp. 2003. "Price and Income Elasticities of Residential Water Demand: A Meta-Analysis." *Land Economics* 79 (2): 292–308.

Damania, R., S. Desbureaux, and E. Zaveri. 2020. "Does Rainfall Matter for Economic Growth? Evidence from Global Sub-national Data (1990–2014)." *Journal of Environmental Economics and Management* 102: 102335.

Dell, M., B. F. Jones, and B. A. Olken. 2014. "What Do We Learn from the Weather? The New Climate–Economy Literature." *Journal of Economic Literature* 52 (3): 740–98.

Demerle, R. 2020. "Smart Water Metering: Digitizing to Survive?" *Water and Wastes Digest*, May 20. https://www.wwdmag.com/advanced-meter-reading -amr/smart-water-metering-digitizing-survive.

Desbureaux, S., and A. S. Rodella. 2017. *Shocks in the Cities: The Economic Impact of Water Shocks in Latin American Metropolitan Areas.* Washington, DC: World Bank.

Douglas, P. M., M. Pagani, M. A. Canuto, M. Brenner, D. A. Hodell, T. I. Eglinton, and J. H. Curtis. 2015. "Drought, Agricultural Adaptation, and Sociopolitical Collapse in the Maya Lowlands." *Proceedings of the National Academy of Sciences* 112 (18): 5607–12.

Dudley, N., and S. Stolton. 2003. *Running Pure: The Importance of Forest Protected Areas to Drinking Water.* Washington, DC: World Bank/WWF Alliance for Forest Conservation and Sustainable Use. https://openknowledge.worldbank .org/handle/10986/15006.

Erlanger, P. D., and B. Neal. 2005. *Framework for Urban Water Resource Planning.* Melbourne: Water Services Association of Australia.

Espey, M., J. Espey, and W. D. Shaw. 1997. "Price Elasticity of Residential Demand for Water: A Meta-Analysis." *Water Resources Research* 33 (6): 1369–74.

Evans, S. T. 2008. "Part IV: Late Classic, Classic Collapse, and Epiclassic." In *Ancient Mexico and Central America: Archaeology and Culture History*, 315–76. London: Thames and Hudson.

FAO (Food and Agriculture Organization of the United Nations). 2018. "Drought Characteristics and Management in North Africa and the Near East." FAO Water Reports No. 45. Rome: FAO.

FAO (Food and Agriculture Organization of the United Nations). AQUASTAT database. FAO, Rome. http://www.fao.org/aquastat/en/.

Farooq, U. 2018. "Will Istanbul's Massive New Canal Be an Environmental Disaster?" *National Geographic*, March 28. https://www.nationalgeographic.com/science/article/istanbul-canal-project-bosporus-environmental-impacts.

Flörke, M., C. Schneider, and R. I. McDonald. 2018. "Water Competition between Cities and Agriculture Driven by Climate Change and Urban Growth." *Nature Sustainability* 1 (1): 51–58.

Fuente, D. 2017. "Essays on Water and Sanitation Service Delivery in Sub-Saharan Africa." Doctoral dissertation, The University of North Carolina at Chapel Hill.

Gabaix, X. 1999. "Zipf's Law for Cities: An Explanation." *Quarterly Journal of Economics* 114 (3): 739–67.

Godfrey, M. 2014. "Desalination Plant at Kurnell Costing Taxpayers $534,246 a Day as It Sits Idle While Water Levels Remain High." *Daily Telegraph*, August 23.

Grafton, R. Q., L. Chu, and T. Kompas. 2015. "Optimal Water Tariffs and Supply Augmentation for Cost-of-Service Regulated Water Utilities." *Utilities Policy* 34: 54–62.

Grant, S. B., J. D. Saphores, D. L. Feldman, A. J. Hamilton, T. D. Fletcher, P. L. M. Cook, M. Stewardson, B. F. Sanders, L. A. Levin, R. F. Ambrose, A. Deletic, R. Brown, S. C. Jiang, D. Rosso, W. J. Cooper, and I. Marusic. 2012. "Taking the 'Waste' out of 'Wastewater' for Human Water Security and Ecosystem Sustainability." *Science* 337 (6095): 681–6.

Hallegatte, S., M. Bangalore, L. Bonzanigo, M. Fay, T. Kane, U. Narloch, J. Rozenberg, D. Treguer, and A. Vogt-Schilb. 2016. *Shock Waves: Managing the Impacts of Climate Change on Poverty*. Washington, DC: World Bank. https://openknowledge.worldbank.org/handle/10986/22787.

Henderson, J. V., A. Storeygard, and D. N. Weil. 2012. "Measuring Economic Growth from Outer Space." *American Economic Review* 102 (2): 994–1028.

IATP (Institute for Agriculture and Trade Policy). 2002. "Worsening Water Shortage Prompts Riots in Algeria." IATP, June 6.

Islam, A., and M. Hyland. 2019. "The Drivers and Impacts of Water Infrastructure Reliability: A Global Analysis of Manufacturing Firms." *Ecological Economics* 163: 143–57.

Istanbul Water and Sewerage Administration. 2012. *2012 Annual Report*. https://www.iski.gov.tr/web/assets/SayfalarDocs/Annual%20Report/2012%20-%20%C4%B0SK%C4%B0%20ANNUAL%20REPORT.pdf.

Jia, C., and G. Anfei. 2010. "Drought Inflicts a Heavy Toll." *China Daily*, February 9. http://www.chinadaily.com.cn/china/2010-02/09/content_9447073.htm

Kettab, A., D. Ait Mouhoub, T. Ouarda, and B. Bobbee. 2004. "Contribution à l'étude du phénomène de la sécheresse sur les régions littorales de l'Algérie." CMURMEI meeting on innovation as a tool for sustainable development within the Mediterranean, Foggia, Italy, October 14.

Blankespoor, B., A. Khan, and H. Selod. 2019. *The Two Tails of Cities. A (More) Exhaustive Perspective on Urban Population Growth and City Spatial Expansion*. Unpublished manuscript.

Kocornik-Mina, A., T. K. McDermott, G. Michaels, and F. Rauch. 2020. "Flooded Cities." *American Economic Journal: Applied Economics* 12 (2): 35–66.

Kotzé, P. 2018. "Post Day Zero: Lessons in Resilience from São Paulo." *Water Wheel* 17 (3): 16–20.

Mahjabin, T., S. Garcia, C. Grady, and A. Mejia. 2018. "Large Cities Get More for Less: Water Footprint Efficiency across the US." *PloS One* 13 (8): e0202301.

Matsuura, K., and C. J. Willmott. 2018. "Terrestrial Air Temperature and Precipitation: Monthly and Annual Time Series (1900–2017)." http://climate.geog.udel.edu/~climate/html_pages/download.html.

McKernan, B. 2021. "Turkey Drought: Istanbul Could Run Out of Water in 45 Days." *The Guardian*, January 13.

Michaels, G., F. Rauch, and S. J. Redding. 2012. "Urbanization and Structural Transformation." *Quarterly Journal of Economics* 127 (2): 535–86.

Miyan, M. A. 2015. "Droughts in Asian Least Developed Countries: Vulnerability and Sustainability." *Weather and Climate Extremes* 7: 8–23.

Moe, C. L., and R. D. Rheingans. 2006. "Global Challenges in Water, Sanitation and Health." *Journal of Water and Health* 4 (S1): 41–57.

Nature Conservancy and R. McDonald. 2016. "City Water Map (Version 2.2)." Knowledge Network for Biocomplexity. doi:10.5063/F1J67DWR.

Nauges, C., and D. Whittington. 2010. "Estimation of Water Demand in Developing Countries: An Overview." *World Bank Research Observer* 25 (2): 263–94.

Naz, F., G. H. Dars, K. Ansari, S. Jamro, and N. Y. Krakauer. 2020. "Drought Trends in Balochistan." *Water* 12 (2): 470.

NDTV. 2019. "Over 1,600 Dead in India's Heaviest Monsoon in 25 Years: Report." *NDTV India*, October 1.

New Humanitarian. 2003. "Guinea: Water and Power Shortages Blamed on Drought." Geneva: *New Humanitarian*.

New Humanitarian. 2010. "Pakistan: Top 10 Natural Disasters since 1935." Geneva: *New Humanitarian*. https://www.thenewhumanitarian.org/news/2010/08/10.

OCHA (United Nations Office for the Coordination of Humanitarian Affairs). 2002. "Drought and Floods in Central America Updated Spring 2002." *Reliefweb*, June 6.

OCHA (United Nations Office for the Coordination of Humanitarian Affairs). 2003. "Guinea: Water and Power Shortages Blamed on Drought." *Reliefweb*, June 5.

Pascale, S., S. B. Kapnick, T. L. Delworth, and W. F. Cooke. 2020. "Increasing Risk of another Cape Town 'Day Zero' Drought in the 21st Century." *Proceedings of the National Academy of Sciences* 117 (47): 29495–503.

Pérez-Urdiales, M., and K. A. Baerenklau. 2020. "Assessing the Impacts of Urban Water-Use Restrictions at the District Level: Case Study of California's Drought Mandate." *Journal of Water Resources Planning and Management* 146 (5): 05020004.

Pontes, R. J., J. Freeman, J. W. Oliveira-Lima, J. C. Hodgson, and A. Spielman. 2000. "Vector Densities That Potentiate Dengue Outbreaks in a Brazilian City." *American Journal of Tropical Medicine and Hygiene* 62: (3): 378–83.

Qiu, J. 2010. "China Drought Highlights Future Climate Threats." *Nature* 465: 142–43.

Quetta District Government. 2011. *Quetta: Integrated District Development Vision*. Quetta, Pakistan: IUCN Pakistan. https://portals.iucn.org/library/node/10183.

Renwick, M. E., and S.O. Archibald. 1998. "Demand Side Management Policies for Residential Water Use: Who Bears the Conservation Burden?" *Land Economics* 74 (3): 343–59.

Rinaudo, J. D., N. Neverre, and M. Montginoul. 2012. "Simulating the Impact of Pricing Policies on Residential Water Demand: A Southern France Case Study." *Water Resources Management* 26 (7): 2057–68. doi:10.1007/s11269 -012-9998-z.

Ritter, K. 2018. "São Paulo Heading to Another Dry Spell." *Circle of Blue*, March 7.

Russ, J. 2020. "Water Runoff and Economic Activity: The Impact of Water Supply Shocks on Growth." *Journal of Environmental Economics and Management* 101: 102322.

Scally, P. 2016. "River Diversion to Flush Pollution out of Yunnan's Dianchi Lake." *The Third Pole*, February 29. https://www.thethirdpole.net/en/pollution /river-diversion-to-flush-pollution-out-of-yunnans-dianchi-lake/.

Sharer, R. J., and L. P. Traxler. 2006. *The Ancient Maya*. Stanford University Press: Redwood City, CA.

Singh, T., and L. S. Kandari. 2012. "Rainwater Harvesting in the Wake of Climate Change: A Case Study from Shimla City, Himachal Pradesh." *Universal Journal of Environmental Research and Technology* 2 (4): 336–46.

Singh, C., G. Jain, V. Sukhwani, and R. Shaw. 2021. "Losses and Damages Associated with Slow-Onset Events: Urban Drought and Water Insecurity in Asia." *Current Opinion in Environmental Sustainability* 50: 72–86.

Smiley, C. H. 1960. "The Antiquity and Precision of Mayan Astronomy." *Journal of the Royal Astronomical Society of Canada* 54: 222.

Storeygard, A. 2016. "Farther on Down the Road: Transport Costs, Trade and Urban Growth in Sub-Saharan Africa." *Review of Economic Studies* 83 (3): 1263–95.

Thilakarathne, M., and V. Sridhar. 2017. "Characterization of Future Drought Conditions in the Lower Mekong River Basin." *Weather and Climate Extremes* 17: 47–58.

Touchan, R., K. J. Anchukaitis, D. M. Meko, S. Attalah, C. Baisan, and A. Aloui. 2008. "Long-Term Context for Recent Drought in Northwestern Africa." *Geophysical Research Letters* 35 (13).

UNESCO (United Nations Educational, Scientific and Cultural Organization). 2018. *Atlas de sequías de América Latina y el Caribe*. Paris: UNESCO Publishing.

Varadhan, S. 2019. "Villagers Accuse City of Seizing Water as Drought Parches 'India's Detroit.'" *Reuters*, July 3.

Ward, C., and S. Ruckstuhl. 2017. *Water Scarcity, Climate Change and Conflict in the Middle East: Securing Livelihoods, Building Peace*. New York: Bloomsbury Publishing.

Watts, G., B. von Christierson, J. Hannaford, and K. Lonsdale. 2012. "Testing the Resilience of Water Supply Systems to Long Droughts." *Journal of Hydrology* 414: 255–67.

World Bank. 2018. "Population Living in Slums (% of Urban Population)." In *World Development Indicators*. Washington, DC: World Bank. https://data .worldbank.org/indicator/EN.POP.SLUM.UR.ZS.

World Bank. World Development Indicators database. World Bank, Washington, DC. http://data.worldbank.org/data-catalog/world-development-indicators.

Worthington, A. C., and M. Hoffman. 2008. "An Empirical Survey of Residential Water Demand Modelling." *Journal of Economic Surveys* 22 (5): 842–71.

Wu, Q., J. Cheng, D. Liu, L. Han, and Y. Yang. 2015. "Kunming: A Regional International Mega City in Southwest China." In *Urban Development Challenges, Risks and Resilience in Asian Mega Cities*, edited by Ram Babu Singh, 323–47. Tokyo: Springer.

Zhao, L., K. Oleson, E. Bou-Zeid, E. S. Krayenhoff, A. Bray, Q. Zhu, Z. Zheng, C. Chen, and M. Oppenheimer. 2021. "Global Multi-model Projections of Local Urban Climates." *Nature Climate Change* 11: 152–7.

CHAPTER FIVE

GOING WITH THE FLOW

> *"Come, my friends,*
> *'Tis not too late to seek a newer world.*
> *Push off, and sitting well in order smite*
> *The sounding furrows"*

— Alfred, Lord Tennyson, "Ulysses"

KEY HIGHLIGHTS

- Policies can target risks at the source of migration (in situ) or at the destination (ex situ).

- None of these policies in isolation is likely to be completely effective at protecting people and their assets. Since residual risks remain, there is a need for synchronized and complementary policies that can cover different dimensions of risk.

- There is no consensus on whether migration is an appropriate strategy of adaptation to chronic risks or whether it represents a failure of risk mitigation policy. Likewise, there is no consensus on the economic impacts at the destination.

- Even so, there is a role for governments at the destination to assist economic and social integration of migrants and to prepare cities for acute bouts of water shortages. Policies should allow for flexibility in responses rather than requiring costly and irreversible investments that risk being unused and becoming stranded assets.

THE POLICY CHALLENGE

This report has demonstrated that the popular image of droughts or floods driving waves of destitute migrants to safer ground is a misleading caricature. The decision to migrate is potentially risky and life changing and has wide ramifications. It is driven by a host of factors that can interact in ways that either offset or reinforce the initial shock. Apart from "push" factors such as natural disasters, the decision to move also depends on whether there are better prospects available elsewhere ("pull" factors) and whether a move is feasible (that is, affordable). And since migration is costly, the evidence suggests that only deep and cumulative water deficits induce statistically discernable movements of people. Even when these shocks occur, those people who are extremely poor may still lack the resources, access to credit, or the networks that would enable a move to a better life elsewhere.

One implication of this finding is that the mass movement of people in poorer regions of the world will differ systematically from observed responses in less poor areas. Where there is extreme poverty, and migration is costly, droughts are more likely to trap households in further poverty and hardship. Conversely, the same rainfall deficit might induce migration in middle-income settings where households can pay for the costs of relocation through savings, borrowing, or liquidating assets (Cattaneo and Peri 2016; Burke and Tanutama 2019; Peri and Sasahara 2019).

Hence this report finds that migration responses differ systematically between low-income and middle-income settings—in the former case, droughts trap households in poverty, while in the latter case, households tend to migrate in response to cumulative dry shocks. Consistent with other research, this report also finds that distress migration occurs in response to rainfall deficits rather than to floods. This finding could be because wet episodes tend to be beneficial in dry rural geographies, while recovery from floods in cities can be quite rapid, with little observable effect on economic activity (Gray and Mueller 2012; Kocornik-Mina et al. 2020; World Bank 2021).

The development implications of these findings seem stark. In the coming decades extreme poverty, more intense drought due to climate change, and violent conflict are likely to increasingly occur in the same places and thus be experienced simultaneously by the same communities. By 2030, upwards of two-thirds of those living in extreme poverty will also be living in fragile, conflict-affected, and vulnerable settings; these also happen to be the most vulnerable regions that will endure the greatest effects of climate change. Under the status quo, these regions are likely to become potential drought traps, where more frequent and severe weather events have adverse impacts on economic performance, while weak economic performance translates into underinvestment in risk reduction. And because of endemic poverty, people will find that escape through migration is also unaffordable. This "triple jeopardy" could lock communities into higher levels of poverty and greater vulnerability, since they lack the resources to overcome migration costs or to adapt to elevated climate threats.

The way in which governments respond to these challenges will either implicitly or explicitly influence decisions to migrate. Placing greater emphasis on policies that promote the integration of migrants at their destination would make migration more attractive, whereas policies that focus on eliminating risks at the source may tacitly discourage migration. The appropriate policy response will likely vary over time and across locations. This suggests that responses can be categorized in terms of those policies that focus on reducing risks or impacts at the source, and those that address concerns that arise at the migrants' destination. Figure 5.1 provides a summary.

Deciding on the appropriate policy response is complex and goes beyond a narrow comparison of the relative costs of different options (Chambwera et al. 2014; Fankhauser 2017). Cost comparisons often fail to adequately account for noneconomic benefits, which are especially important when dealing with social and environmental concerns. For instance, this omission can bias decisions against the maintenance of environmental assets whose functions are neither well understood nor adequately captured in valuation exercises. Biodiversity and watershed benefits would be prominent examples in this category. Second, as emphasized later in this chapter, when there are information asymmetries or coordination failures (or nonconvexities), a decision based on a comparison of costs will not be sufficient to determine whether migration is adaptive or maladaptive. Third, migration, as do policies to address risks, has social and distributional consequences. Who gains and who loses may matter, and some policies may have (unintended) regressive consequences that will not be captured in a monetary comparison of costs. Finally, dynamic considerations are also involved. Policy choices influence where people live. As the population of a given location grows, policy support may become necessary for social well-being despite high

FIGURE 5.1: **Policy Approaches at the Source and Destination**

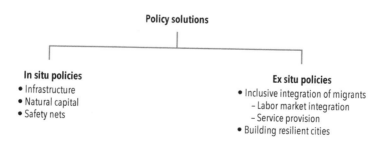

Source: World Bank.

environmental and economic costs. Over time well-intentioned investments can generate costly lock-in effects due to such path dependence. Additionally, perverse incentives due to moral hazard problems might undermine policy objectives. With climate change comes even greater uncertainty about what the future will hold. Such circumstances put a high premium on adaptable and flexible approaches that can respond to new information and changing circumstances (see box 5.1).

POLICY OPTIONS AT THE ORIGIN

Policy impacts will vary by location, but broadly the choice of policies to buffer resident communities from droughts in situ would need to be selected from three broad categories: (a) built physical infrastructure, such as large multipurpose dams or small storage options and other investments in timely and accurate meteorological and hydrological information; (b) green natural infrastructure that physically protects and may also provide drought-proof

BOX 5.1: Analytical Approaches Help Decision-Makers Confront Large Uncertainties

Uncertainty is intrinsic to decision-making. This is even truer in the case of water management decisions under climate change: projections of water supply and demand are characterized by large, irreducible uncertainties. Projections of water supply, for example, typically rely on climate models that quantify temperature and rainfall conditions several decades into the future. Even as the science continues to evolve and new generations of climate models improve on existing models, considerable uncertainties in climate projections remain. While all climate models tend to agree that the future will be warmer (that is, increasing in temperature), there is considerable uncertainty in projections of future rainfall conditions (Niang et al. 2014). For many parts of the world, particularly the tropics, there is little agreement as to the trend and magnitude of future rainfall (James and Washington 2013; Zaveri et al. 2016).

In Africa, for example, rainfall projections show high variation between climate models in both the magnitude and direction of change, partly due to the inability of these models to represent complex atmospheric processes in tropical regions (figure 5A.1.1 in annex 5A). By the end of the century, the likely change in rainfall in Africa could span anywhere from −4.3 percent to 65.4 percent, depending on the chosen set of scenarios or shared socioeconomic pathways that cover a range of plausible

box continues next page

BOX 5.1: Analytical Approaches Help Decision-Makers Confront Large Uncertainties *continued*

socioeconomic trends and climate mitigation targets. As this report has shown, there is also uncertainty about some of the social and economic consequences of rainfall shocks. This uncertainty makes it difficult to know what to plan for.

The recognition of this uncertainty has given rise to a range of methods for decision making under "deep" uncertainty, such as robust decision making, decision scaling, vulnerability analysis, and dynamic adaptive policy pathways (Hallegatte et al. 2012). While these approaches differ in their specifics, they are all based on a shared set of principles (Borgomeo et al. 2018). First, they identify conditions under which the performance of the water investment becomes unacceptable before assigning probabilities to these conditions. Second, they focus on robust decisions, broadly defined as decisions that perform acceptably well under a wide range of plausible future conditions (such as rainfall patterns well beyond those observed in the historical record), rather than decisions that perform optimally over a narrow set of conditions (such as historical rainfall patterns). Third, decision making under uncertainty highlights the importance of flexibility in water investments—that is, the ability to switch or change a decision depending on what outcomes materialize and what new information becomes available. Fourth, they strongly emphasize the multiobjective nature of all water investments and the need to explore the trade-offs between these multiple objectives under uncertainty.

The World Bank is increasingly adopting these analytical approaches to inform its investments and support its clients in pursuing water security and broader resilience to climate change. For example, the World Bank helped Lima's water utility refine its water supply master plan and identify necessary investments and components to achieve water reliability by 2040, regardless of future climate and demand (Groves et al. 2019). It also supported the prioritization of hydropower investments in the Koshi Basin of Nepal, identifying robust investment portfolios amid uncertainties: glacier melts, electricity prices, and export opportunities (World Bank 2015). The World Bank has also developed guidelines to help water planners and project managers ensure that investments and designs are resilient in the face of uncertainty. These guidelines include the Decision Tree Framework, *Building the Resilience of Water Supply and Sanitation Utilities to Climate Change and Other Threats: A Roadmap* (World Bank 2018a), and the Resilient Water Infrastructure Design Brief (World Bank 2020).

sources of income along with investments in climate-smart agriculture; and (c) other "soft" policy options, such as safety nets that can provide income and livelihood buffers when shocks occur.

Storage Solutions

Water storage and supplemental irrigation are the most commonly used solutions to buffer rural communities against water variability and scarcity. And indeed there is much evidence to show that on average such interventions are effective and necessary to protect vulnerable rural communities. But there are caveats that suggest the need for more closely examining the effectiveness of interventions.

An emerging body of evidence shows that in many cases, such investments have provided short-term relief, but they have also created moral hazard problems that have undermined the policy objectives. In the North American Great Plains, when access to groundwater was made available, farmers shifted to more water-intensive crops that ultimately increased drought vulnerability (Hornbeck and Keskin 2014). Similarly, in the western United States, dams initially helped to smooth production during drought but over time also incentivized farmers to grow higher-value crops that were water intensive, which eventually made their income even more volatile in times of drought (Hansen, Libecap, and Lowe 2011). Thus, while both groundwater and surface water storage solutions may offer critical benefits to reducing vulnerability, caution must be exercised in overstating the long-term consequences.

The reasons for this are widely understood. When irrigation water supplies are provided at little or no charge, this sends an economic signal that water is abundant—even when it is scarce. In response to these economic signals, water is overused and farming turns to water-intensive crops. The result is that there is no buffer left for lean times when there are consecutive years of drought. Accordingly, chapter 2 of this volume finds that in these regions, despite the presence of irrigation infrastructure, a "drought trap" emerges, with irrigation no longer providing long-run resilience to drought. Over time, these conditions increase drought vulnerability such that the incentives to migrate increase.

One implication is that the investments are necessary, but they need to be combined with regulations (such as rationing water or pricing water) to promote more judicious use. In practice, pricing irrigation water at its scarcity value has proved to be challenging and may not be feasible in low-income countries where institutions are weak and low farm productivity restricts the ability to pay for water. Quantity controls (such as water rationing) may carry fewer administrative burdens, but evidence suggests that regulations are routinely evaded where governance is weak.[1] Hence in drought-prone and weak institutional settings where reform is challenging, built infrastructure would need to be complemented with other safeguards that recognize these regulatory limitations.

Without proper safeguards, such investments can paradoxically also increase exposure to other risks, such as the likelihood of conflict breaking out. A large literature has documented the existence of links between heightened water scarcity and conflict (Miguel, Satyanath, and Sergenti 2004; Harari and Ferrara 2018; Acemoglu, Fergusson, and Johnson 2020).[2] What may be surprising, however, is that an abundance of water can at times also bring with it the curse of conflict.

New evidence suggests that large-scale irrigation investments in some locations can become magnets for conflict. This is especially true in regions with a history of conflict between groups and during periods of heightened fragility. For instance, the evidence reflected in figure 5.2 shows that after the disruptions caused during the Arab Spring, irrigated regions of North Africa and the G5 Sahel countries (Burkina Faso, Chad, Mali, Mauritania, and Niger) experienced higher incidence of conflict in irrigated areas (for details, see the technical appendix to this report, available at www.worldbank.org /ebbflow and Khan and Rodella, forthcoming). Conflict in this study is measured by the occurrence of riots and protests, or battles between rebel groups and government forces.

There are many channels through which the changes brought by irrigation investments can make land more prone to conflict risks. In resource-scarce settings such as those found in desert climates, historical codependence has led to the evolution of informal institutional arrangements that establish rules and customs for the sharing of natural resources across diverse groups such as farmers and migratory herders. Sudden shifts in demographic and economic pressures can throw off this delicate balance. For instance, increased population densities and agricultural expansion that accompany irrigation can heighten competition for scarce local resources such as land. If the changes brought by investment amplify inequality, this condition would further fuel grievances of displaced and excluded persons (typically nomadic herders in this case). The new wealth created would also paradoxically make irrigated areas a more lucrative target for pillaging, especially if perceptions of exclusion amplify grievances.

Indeed, the value generated by investments such as irrigation is critical to development, which suggests the importance of better understanding how these investments inadvertently alter the social balance and economic incentives of a region. This knowledge is especially important in regions where livelihood options are limited and there is a history of conflict, such as the agropastoral conflicts in the Sahel. Here the links with water, climate, and migration also come into stark focus. These conflicts are found to be rooted in the disturbance of seasonal migration patterns by rainfall deficits and the pursuant encroachment of farmers' land and water resources by displaced pastoralists and their herds (McGuirk and Nunn 2020).

FIGURE 5.2: Share of Regions in North Africa and G5 Sahel Countries That Experienced Different Types of Conflict Events, by the Presence of Irrigation

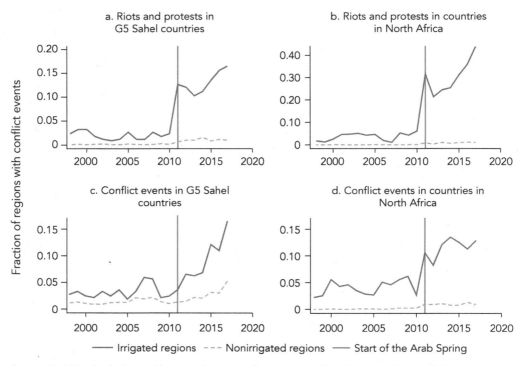

Source: World Bank calculations based on data on conflict occurrence from the Armed Conflict & Event Data Project (ACLED), https://www.acleddata.com, and data on irrigation presence from Siebert et al. 2015.
Note: The five G5 Sahel countries are Burkina Faso, Chad, Mali, Mauritania, and Niger. North Africa refers to Algeria, Djibouti, Arab Republic of Egypt, Libya, Morocco, and Tunisia. The green line indicates 2011, the start of the Arab Spring.

One implication of this finding is that policy decisions that alter access to shared resources may need to be accompanied by complementary investments in effective social protection systems—such as the World Bank's Sahel Adaptive Social Protection Program (World Bank 2018b)—for the poorest and most vulnerable populations. Additionally, this finding also highlights the need for infrastructure investments to be tailored to local and historical contexts. As interventions like farmer-led irrigation development are implemented they can leverage traditional local knowledge to inform more resilient investments.

Hydromet Services

Another important means of mitigating the consequences of weather fluctuations for populations at the source are accurate and timely climate, weather, and water resources information. Weather forecasting is an example of a technology-intensive public good that has minimal delivery costs and that can substantially reduce the principal source of income risk for poor households. Like actuarially fair insurance, better medium-term and seasonal forecasts can guide farmers' choices about when or what to plant, and when to irrigate or fertilize—a strategy that can cut crop losses and raise incomes, and that also can counteract some of the added uncertainty climate change brings (Browder et al. 2021). In countries like India, expected total gains from a correct forecast could reach over 29 billion rupees due to increases in farm profitability (Rosenzweig and Udry 2019). The returns to enhancing individual risk reduction by improving the accuracy of annual and interannual weather forecasts are thus potentially high, given the small costs of delivery.

Nature-Based Solutions

Green infrastructure can play a vital role in providing resilience to drought as well as flood protection. Forests and their associated watersheds store, filter, and gradually distribute both surface water and groundwater, and as a result enhance the resilience and quality of water supplies. In addition, forests are an important source of drought-proof income for rural poor households. Evidence suggests that the very poorest individuals obtain a greater proportion (around 25–30 percent) of their incomes from forest resources than from agriculture (Angelsen et al. 2014; Damania, Joshi, and Russ 2020). Importantly, their dependence on forest resources increases during times of drought, suggesting that forests act as a safety net—nature's social security check—in times of need.

As demonstrated by new analysis in chapter 2 of this volume, in areas where forest cover is high, out-migration in response to droughts is low or negligible. Estimates further suggest that nature-based solutions are cost-effective: on average it would cost about US$0.8 trillion to US$3 trillion in irrigation infrastructure to compensate for a 10 percentage point decrease in the share of forested land to restore the buffering effects of natural capital lost because of deforestation. Other studies have shown that preserving floodplains can reduce flood damage by up to 78 percent and that using environmentally sensitive agricultural and land management practices can increase water flows. Investing in complementary solutions to buffer incomes—for example, protecting watersheds and forests, together with a canal or dam for irrigation—produces greater benefits than investing in any single one of these solutions (Guannel et al. 2016).

These estimates highlight the important role of nature-based solutions. They are environmentally beneficial and socially benign, and they involve no large-scale resettlement. In addition, financial outlays are limited or negligible, which is especially important in the COVID-19 context, in which fiscal space is limited and debt is rising.

Climate-Smart Agriculture

A related and critically important approach to buffer rural livelihoods from climate change and increasing rainfall variability is climate-smart agriculture (CSA). CSA combines smart policies, financing, and technologies to achieve a triple win—increasing productivity, enhancing resilience, and reducing greenhouse gas emissions (World Bank and International Energy Agency 2015). CSA emphasizes that any efforts to intensify food production must be matched by a concerted focus on making it sustainable because failing to do so could undermine the capacity for future growth. Policies that encourage farmer-led irrigation can also ensure that small- and larger-holder farmers alike can reap the benefits of irrigation investments, building resilience against climate and economic shocks in a more inclusive and sustainable way.

Adopting CSA is especially critical in light of recent evidence that suggests that despite important agricultural advancements to feed the world in the past 60 years, global farming productivity has slumped by 21 percent since 1961, compared with a world without climate change, because of an escalation in climate sensitivity in recent years (Ortiz-Bobea et al. 2021). Embracing a climate-smart food systems is, therefore, necessary to avoid further damage to livelihoods and could go a long way toward minimizing the environmental footprint by reducing water wastage, overuse, and pollution.

Safety Nets

Evidence coming from multiple studies across different geographies consistently shows that in poor rural areas the deprivations caused by droughts impede the development of young children who experience them in their critical early years of growth. The children grow up shorter, less educated, and less wealthy (Maccini and Yang 2009; Almond and Currie 2011). In some cases the deprivations may be transmitted to the next generation (Hyland and Russ 2019). The provision of irrigation infrastructure and natural capital solutions may provide buffers that reduce the impacts of drought. But inevitably some residual risks will remain, even in advanced systems. Managing these residual impacts is important to avoid the permanent and potentially intergenerational consequences of drought. Adaptive safety nets can play a key role in achieving better outcomes.

Safety net programs, such as cash and in-kind transfers, have long been used to provide a minimum level of support to those in need, both during normal times and in times of crisis. Those programs are also increasingly combined with measures aimed at improving human development outcomes, for instance in nutrition and childcare. Addressing the types of shocks and irreversible impacts identified in this report would mean implementing programs that target vulnerable populations most in need. In practical terms, this might mean designing programs that cover only the poorest of the population, or those who are chronically food insecure, with geographic targeting in areas where rainfall shocks are most frequent. These approaches will always be challenging because of risks of capture, exclusion (counting as nonpoor individuals or households that are poor), leakage (counting as poor those that are not), limited knowledge, and capacity constraints. Safety net benefits can also be universal and available to all households, eliminating some of the difficulty of targeting households but increasing the costs of the program.

Not surprisingly, universal subsidies are costly, and the fiscal strains associated with them erode the level of program benefits and their effectiveness. Hence, most programs in developing countries are targeted. But a recent review of safety nets in developing countries found that targeting is typically imprecise and that few programs are set up to assist households managing idiosyncratic shocks (Monchuk 2013).

An insurance-based approach is another scheme that may be useful. But it should be noted that determining insurance payout triggers and amounts is often difficult, especially in poor rural areas. One solution is a weather index insurance scheme, whereby payouts are based on triggers that are correlates of losses, rather than actual losses of individuals or area losses themselves. For example, payment of a known sum might be triggered by satellite data on rainfall or satellite imagery measuring the blueness of the ground as a proxy for the degree of flooding. Recent advances in crop modeling and remote sensing—especially in the availability and use of high-resolution imagery from satellites that can pinpoint individual areas—can go a long way to improve the quality of index insurance by strengthening the link between indices and actual losses, as well as by reducing program costs (Benami et al. 2021).

An advantage of this approach is that in times of need, there is an automatic payout with little room for fraudulent manipulation. The main disadvantage is the risk that a payout might not be made even though a loss has occurred, or that a payout might be made even when there is no loss. Given the depth of the consequences of delaying action to mitigate the impact of water shocks, the risks of errors of exclusion (triggering insurance in the absence of a disaster) may well be outweighed by the benefits of a more generous system. Secondary audits that allow people to present their claims of losses that the index failed to detect could also be put into place to minimize uncompensated losses due to index errors. Smartphones, drones, and other technological advances can offer further possibilities to reduce the cost of these audits (Benami et al. 2021).

POLICY OPTIONS AT THE DESTINATION

While droughts trap poor people in low-income countries, they tend to induce waves of migration in middle-income countries, at a scale not experienced in normal times. This has implications for the destination and raises questions about the appropriate policy responses. As with policies at the source, options for easing transitions at the migration destination—typically, cities—will be contextual and will vary by location. Nevertheless, there are two main areas in which decision-makers could focus: (a) economically integrating migrants into communities to both limit impacts on host communities and ensure inclusive opportunities for new migrants; and (b) transforming these cities to make them more resilient to water shocks of their own.

Inclusive Integration of Migrants

The evidence presented in chapter 3 of this volume indicates that drought migrants in middle-income countries tend to be less educated than the average migrants who move to their host city otherwise. This situation raises concerns that a large influx of people seeking work would create competition for jobs with negative wage impacts at the lower end of the labor market. For instance, Lall, Timmins, and Yu (2009) find that although migration may improve the welfare of the migrants, migration tends to add to congestion costs in cities and, as a result, the economy may end up worse off. In this case there is a need for policies that build human capital and improve access to water, sanitation, health, and education.

However, it is also possible that beneficial effects may arise from the stimulus to demand for housing and other nontradable goods and services. Similarly, if immigrant workers bring to the labor market complementary skills, their arrival could yield net economic benefits, such as when migrant enclaves create new industries or bring new skills. There would also be distributional consequences. Wages might decrease for workers affected by the influx of labor, while the increased demand for housing could lead to higher rents and hence transfers from renters to landowners. The overall economic effect is a priori ambiguous and will be determined by local conditions and the capacity of the destination to absorb a larger labor force of lower-skilled workers.

Responding to these problems is especially challenging for city authorities. A city mayor cannot know in advance when the next drought might occur and whether it would generate a wave of migrants; thus preemptive planning is difficult. Instead, attention could turn to helping the migrants integrate socially and economically. The precise policy mix will vary across countries, but the fundamental ingredients would likely remain the same: active labor market policies that build skills through various support and training modalities (such as "schools beyond walls") and that integrate migrants into labor markets are important. Poor migrants who live in informal settlements often endure high levels of violence and insecurity; lack basic services such as water supply and sanitation, schools, and health care; and reside in unsafe housing. Efforts might be made to improve services, to the extent feasible. In the COVID-19 context particular attention to health and water supply and sanitation seems warranted. Basic water and sanitation services are important in slowing the spread of diseases, including COVID-19.

When significant waves of migrants arrive, their presence becomes more visible and is often controversial, and the debates may become ideological. As discussed in "Spotlight: Inequality, Social Cohesion, and the COVID-19 Public Health Crisis at the Nexus of Water and Migration" (see chapter 1 of this volume), such stress during times of large negative shocks has the potential to erupt into social conflict, especially when it exacerbates existing inequalities. Notwithstanding the many unresolved questions and complexities, there seems to be a compelling case for proactive policies that promote shared economic progress and that address social frictions.

Building Resilient Cities

As cities grow at breakneck speed, water services are also increasingly being strained to keep pace with growing populations and increased per capita demand for water. At the same time, climate change is accentuating these challenges and loosening the bounds of the possible by altering the global hydrological cycle, increasing the number of extreme episodes, and making water supplies less predictable. From São Paulo, Brazil, to Cape Town, South Africa, to Chennai, India, millions of city residents find themselves short of water and have come precariously close to "day zero" events, when water supplies become threateningly low. But even as day zero events in these megacities grab international headlines, scores of small cities throughout the developed and developing world alike face similar water shortages. Add to this underlying challenge a sudden influx of new residents during a drought, and the water demand–supply imbalance becomes even more severe.

Understanding the impacts of such water shortages on overall growth has, so far, been achingly elusive, but new evidence discussed in chapter 4 of this volume shows that the impacts can significantly slow urban growth. Depending on the size of the water shock, city growth can slow by nearly 12 percentage points during drought years, enough to reverse critical development progress.

There is no simple solution to addressing these water shortages in cities, but smart policies can reduce their propensity for damage and their impacts. Cities have the potential to stanch future catastrophes by **rethinking urban planning** (see box 5.2). Increasing water supplies through desalination or other supply-augmenting technologies may seem like a quick fix, but history shows that these endeavors can be risky and inefficient. This lesson was learned by the city of Sydney, Australia, which, after facing a severe and extended water shortage, invested in a large and costly desalination plant only to find that by the time the plant was operational the drought had ended and the plant was no longer needed.

Water reallocation may offer another solution for ever-thirstier cities. A recent study showed that, globally, 69 urban areas are receiving water through reallocation projects whereby water is typically transferred to urban areas from surrounding rural areas, often at the expense of agriculture (Garrick et al. 2019). This can occur in several different ways. Reallocation through land use change can occur when donor regions urbanize, thereby organically and somewhat inconspicuously reallocating water from agricultural to urban uses. More disruptive is when water is transported over large areas from one basin to another. As estimated by Garrick et al. (2019), these transfers involve moving an estimated 16 billion cubic

BOX 5.2: New Ideas to Thwart the Next Urban Water Crisis

The world's cities increasingly have to face the difficult task of meeting the rising demands of urban residents in a sustainable way. A new data-driven application, the Advanced Practices for Environmental Excellence in Cities (APEX) app by the International Finance Corporation, is currently being piloted in select cities around the world to meet this challenge (Kapoor 2021).[a] The app allows city planners to make cities more sustainable in four key areas—energy, water, waste, and public transport. It harnesses data insights from advanced green practices around the world to create tailored solutions for cities. The APEX app shows, for example, that it is possible for a city such as Chennai to increase water security by 40 percent by 2050 if it adopted the Singapore model of water management,[b] thus bolstering water self-sufficiency and reducing water bills (Kapoor 2021). City leadership can use the app to measure the potential of making incremental improvements. It can estimate the cost of each solution, the amount of carbon emissions that can be reduced, and the number of jobs that can be added to the local economy by adopting new practices (Kapoor 2021).

Another emerging idea, from China, is to build cities like sponges so that they are capable of absorbing rainwater (Chan et al. 2018). The system is intended to mimic the natural hydrological cycle and is designed to passively absorb, clean, and use

box continues next page

BOX 5.2: **New Ideas to Thwart the Next Urban Water Crisis** *continued*

rainfall in an ecologically friendly way. The idea focuses on restoring wetlands and building green infrastructure to retain and store water. Methods include the use of permeable material in paving, establishment of rooftop gardens, and the creation of storage ponds and areas of wetland. The goal for such cities is not only to be capable of dealing with a sudden excess of stormwater but also to reuse it to help mitigate the impact of droughts. Other cobenefits include contiguous open green spaces, interconnected waterways, and urban wildlife habitats, which, together with less use of concrete, would mean a lower carbon footprint.

As the challenge mounts to absorb the growing demands of urban populations, and as shocks to water supplies increase, city planners will increasingly need to rethink urban planning to ensure that cities remain the engines of economic growth that they have become.

a. The APEX website is https://www.apexcities.com/.
b. The Singapore model embraces a four-tap model. The first tap is the supply of water from local catchments. Most of the city is designed as a catchment with an integrated system of reservoirs and an extensive drainage system that collects rainwater and channels it into storage reservoirs. From the storage reservoirs, water treatment plants treat the rainwater to be supplied to the city as potable water. The second tap is imported water, which supplements Singapore's needs. The third tap is treated wastewater or, as Singapore calls it, NEWater. Wastewater is treated to such high standards that it can be drunk. The fourth tap is desalination. Water from the sea is desalinated and supplied to the city. For the simulation in the APEX app, the first and third taps are assumed.

meters of water nearly 13,000 kilometers. Key to enabling these transfers is investments in efficient use of irrigation water and reuse of wastewater in irrigation, to enable agricultural areas to grow more with less water. A recent estimate by Flörke, Schneider, and McDonald (2018) found that a 10 percent increase in irrigation water use efficiency could free up enough water to reduce urban water deficits by 2.7 billion cubic meters by 2050. Nevertheless, questions still remain on how truly effective, equitable, and sustainable water reallocation is. While in some contexts it may be a critical tool for addressing urban water crises, it will not be a panacea.

Dealing with day zero events, tail risks that occur with non-zero but low probability, is difficult. Water reallocation from rural areas is costly because of the high cost of transporting water, and it is politically complex since it entails depriving farmers of a crucial livelihood resource and input. Creating additional sources of water supply might involve building reservoirs with large storage capacity, or desalination units. These options also have high capital, maintenance, and environmental costs. Moreover because the extreme deficits created by day zero events are rare, the extra supply made available through increased storage or desalination infrastructure may never be needed during the lifespan of these assets. The risk of wasteful investment is inevitably high, with high opportunity costs in developing countries with mounting debts and tightening fiscal space. What is needed is a flexible approach that allows for emergency transfers of water when they are needed.

A "drought option" contract is one way of insuring against extreme drought without the downside risk of investing in obsolete infrastructure. A drought option would give a city the right to buy a specified quantity of water at an agreed price in the event of a drought. The option would only be exercised under agreed weather conditions, which would preserve the water for agriculture during normal situations. This approach would be economically more efficient whenever the marginal forgone benefit of farming is less than the cost of building new infrastructure—a condition that is likely to hold in most circumstances. It would also be more attractive in areas where water deficits are worsening and where new supplies must draw on more distant and more capital-intensive and environmentally costly options. Finally, since the transactions are voluntary, both buyer and seller can expect to benefit from the exchange.

In the absence of such legal arrangements, transfers of water from rural areas have in some cases been coercive. For instance, when confronted by intermittent water supply, cities like Chennai draw on water resources from neighboring rural districts, often at the expense of farming communities fueling tensions between the urban and rural sectors (Varadhan 2019; Singh et al. 2021).

Despite the advantages afforded by option contracts, they are still rare and do not exist in developing countries. That absence suggests the need for capacity building to create the legal and institutional preconditions and for greater research to identify and address other constraints.

Demand-side management might offer another way forward that is also less costly and less risky than supply-side measures. Dynamically efficient volumetric water pricing, for instance, can adjust the price of water to better match the scarcity that cities are facing. By allowing utilities to carefully adjust the price of water on the basis of its scarcity, utilities can avoid the need to invest in water-augmenting technologies and thus save money, reduce water footprints, and keep water costs lower in the long run. Other technologies, such as smart water meters and water-saving and water-reusing appliances, offer ways to help households reduce their water footprint with little sacrifice.

In sum, policies that focus on reducing the adverse impacts of water shocks must be complemented by strategies to build the long-term resilience of communities. Figure 5.3 summarizes the various policy options across the rural–urban continuum. Ultimately, there is no single policy approach that will fit all situations, and it will be particularly important to ensure that local circumstances and local perspectives play a central role in assessing the best policy choices.

FIGURE 5.3: Policies and Investments to Sustain Prosperity

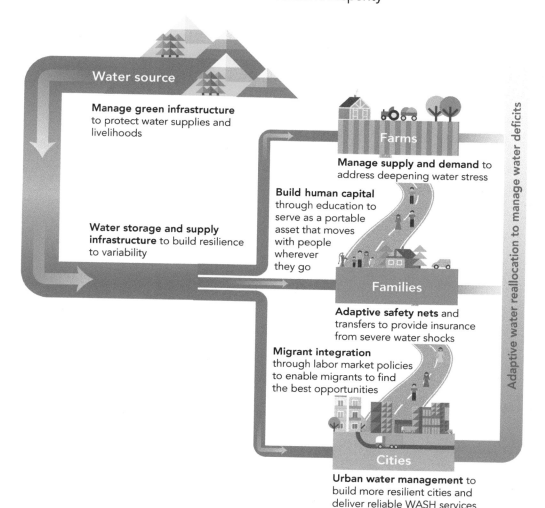

Source: World Bank.
Note: WASH = water, sanitation, and hygiene.

WEIGHING POLICY OPTIONS

With limited resources, governments need to choose policies that are most effective in dealing with the adverse consequences of rainfall-induced migration, especially in the fiscally constrained post-COVID-19 context. There is no consensus on whether climate-induced migration should be viewed as a beneficial long-term adaptation strategy or as a net drain on the resources of destination cities. For policy makers and migrants alike, it will be difficult to predict the eventual outcome of the decision to migrate.

Where there is imperfect information, a move that may be deemed undesirable ex ante might prove to be highly beneficial ex post, and vice versa. Moreover, there could be economies of scope in migration, such that the benefits of migration increase with the numbers that move—for example, when a community builds an identifiable business niche. In this case the push of a drought, not unlike the "big push" theory of development economics,[3] could be the catalyst for movement that unleashes opportunities at the destination that otherwise would not have emerged.

Conversely, it is argued that the lower productivity of migrants escaping droughts has net negative effects on the destination cities, resulting in urbanization without growth. Somewhat controversially, it has been suggested that there is an optimum mix and number of migrants determined by the skills mix and absorptive capacity of host nations (Collier 2013).

Overall generalizations are likely to be misleading, because these are empirical issues for which outcomes will likely vary across countries, and over time as migrants settle and become integrated into the economic and social fabric of their hosts. Notwithstanding the balance of benefits and costs, there remain compelling reasons for destination cities to create the enabling environment that would allow for easier integration into both communities and the local economy (Clemens and Mendola 2020).

This report has also suggested the need for complementary policies, recognizing that no single policy can adequately address the many impacts of a rainfall shock. For instance, infrastructure, while essential, will not be fully effective in eliminating all risks to incomes and well-being. To address these residual risks to incomes might call for safety nets, especially for the most vulnerable. And while a safety net may provide minimum resources necessary for survival, it would not provide the protection for assets and businesses that may be required to spur investment in the affected areas. In such circumstances, infrastructure and safety nets combined would be more effective in drought-proofing communities.

In dealing with migration policies, governments will find inevitable circumstances when they will need to grapple with problems of whether to support people directly or to support the places where people live by enhancing economic opportunities. One of the longest-standing debates in urban economics is between "place-based" policies that are focused on reducing vulnerability and increasing productivity of the places where people reside and "people-based" policies that are focused on assisting vulnerable people (box 5.3).

This question of which policy to pursue is not an easy one, and answers will likely depend on the main drivers and causes of vulnerability. In general, economists have argued that place-based strategies are a blunt instrument for addressing poverty and vulnerability for at least two reasons (Glaeser 2005). First, the policies may be regressive. For instance, a place-based policy that increases land values will benefit richer landowners, and there are risks of elite-capture of land and water resources when such land is developed in otherwise low-productivity contexts. The second concern is that place-based policy may inadvertently worsen problems and lock poor people into places that have limited economic prospects and distort their location decisions. By contrast, people-based policies that are based on personal circumstances will be targeted to needs and will allow residents of disadvantaged areas to move, if they prefer, to better opportunities without losing assistance. Instead of tying assistance to a location, it may be more efficient to target it to the people in need.

BOX 5.3: Place-Based Policies and Risk Management

In general, policy can deal with risk by avoiding the impacts of adverse shocks, mitigating the losses from their occurrence, or transferring the risk—say, via insurance markets (Ehrlich and Becker 1972). But context matters in determining the optimal strategy, such as the density of the location being targeted. Policy makers must be cautious in assuming that a given set of policies can yield equal success in all locales, and they must weigh the costs and benefits of place-based investments. Given the large, upfront costs of many of these investments, and the often long-lasting nature of the assets, it is critical that the choice of places getting the intervention is informed by a realistic, objective, and systematic appraisal of policies (Lall, Maloney, and Grover 2021).

The first step in the appraisal process is to correctly diagnose why certain regions are being held back, and to ascertain whether a place has a latent source of comparative advantage waiting to be unlocked, is reeling from a bad shock but can recover, or is, in fact, nonviable (Lall, Maloney, and Grover 2021). For instance, if sluggish migration traps people in nonviable places, the focus should be on removing barriers to mobility rather than on place-based policies (Lall, Maloney, and Grover 2021). As highlighted in chapter 2 of this volume, poor countries face a host of market frictions that can deter mobility. In addition to restricted budgets that make it costly to migrate in response to droughts, implicit barriers from residency-based access to public services and safety nets, informational asymmetry and distortions in land, and housing markets can also deter mobility.

Equally important is to understand the difficult trade-offs that such interventions involve. Place-based policies that may be socially optimal may not maximize overall welfare. For instance, diverting resources to a region with limited potential for growth from other high-potential regions may address equity concerns in the short run but could reduce growth and welfare over the longer term. Investments also need to be carefully designed to avoid moral hazard that can reduce incentives for risk reduction efforts or encourage building in areas that are clearly exposed to high climatic risk (Lall, Maloney, and Grover 2021). In such instances, providing incentives for people to move or making targeted fiscal transfers may be more beneficial. At the same time,

box continues next page

BOX 5.3: Place-Based Policies and Risk Management *continued*

providing public goods or addressing market failure in places that *are* viable but held back by negative shocks can be transformative.

Since governments face hard budget constraints, prioritization of place-based policies relative to other complementary policies that target individuals, economic sectors, or institutions must be based on sound diagnostics to ensure that resources are allocated efficiently.

Table B5.3.1 presents a typology of possible options for location-specific risk management strategies, contingent on the type of settlement under consideration (Lall and Deichmann 2010). Migration is a risk-avoidance strategy but is less likely to be employed by residents of larger cities. As discussed before, larger cities tend to persist, and their residents are less likely to move out after disasters. For mitigation options, cost-benefit analyses need to account for location growth and net migration dynamics. For the smallest settlements, the benefits of mitigation are usually not found to be worth the costs. Transferring risks to the market is feasible only for the largest cities, since in this case the size of the market can be large enough to incentivize the private provision of insurance.

Distributional implications also arise here, as the less-developed settlements also tend to house the poorest and most vulnerable populations. In the face of disasters such as droughts, poverty reduction may entail short-term mitigation measures such as social safety nets or even provision of infrastructure such as water storage.

Table B5.3.1: Typology of Options for Risk Management

Settlement type	Avoid or migrate	Mitigate losses	Transfer risk or insure
Primate or "Superstar" cities	✗ *persistence*	✓	✗
Secondary cities	✓	✓	✗ *coordination failure*
Small towns and rural areas	✓	✗ *costs exceed benefits*	✗ *coordination failure*

Source: Lall and Deichmann 2010.

There is a consensus that where vulnerabilities arise from underinvestment in public goods and infrastructure, the case is clear for assistance that directly addresses these deficiencies. There may also be a need to address distributional policies through place-based approaches when universal safety nets are unaffordable.

The persistence of place-based regional policy and the many attempts to address problems in lagging regions suggest that there are significant policy and political challenges in targeting aid to people and not places. In principle, the appropriate policy should depend on the cause of the problem. When poverty and vulnerability derive from individual circumstances, then targeting individuals through social assistance and safety nets would be the more effective strategy, and place-based policies would be second best. But where the problem stems from the underprovision of vital public goods such as sanitation, water, canals, and dams, place-based policies may be more appropriate.

More complex are regions with low productivity, where economic potential could be worsened by climate change and the increased demands of a growing population. In such circumstances place-based policies would be less efficient but could still be socially necessary. In this case, the focus could be on providing vital services such as water, sanitation, education, and health to protect and build human capital without the risks of locking people into locations with limited economic potential.

PROJECTED CHANGES IN ANNUAL RAINFALL IN AFRICA

FIGURE 5A.1.1: Projected Changes in Annual Rainfall in Africa

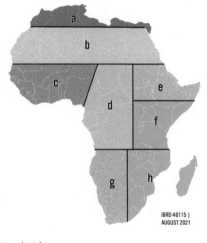

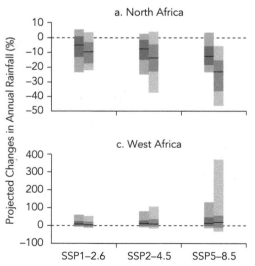

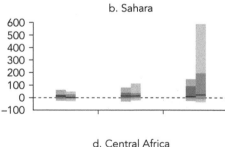

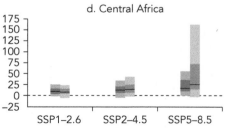

figure continues next page

FIGURE 5A.1.1: **Projected Changes in Annual Rainfall in Africa** continued

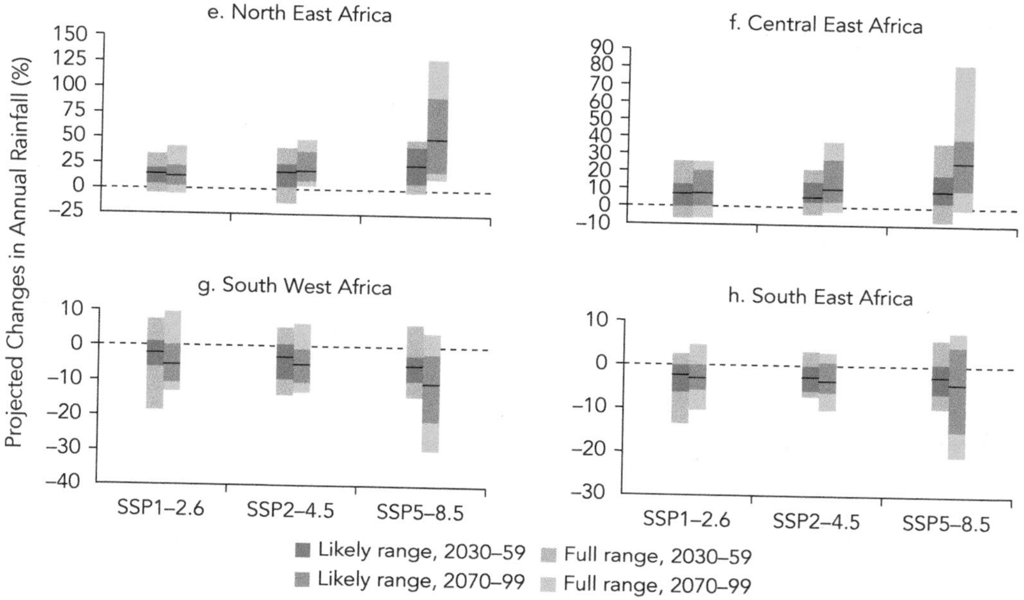

Source: Adapted from Almazroui et al. 2020. Used under the Creative Commons Attribution International License 4.0, https://creativecommons.org/licenses/by/4.0/.

Note: Blue and orange bars represent the results for the near term (2030–59) and long term (2070–99), respectively, for the three scenarios (SSP1-2.6, SSP2-4.5, SSP5-8.5). The length of the bars shows full ranges (results from all the models), and the darker color shows likely ranges (66 percent of all projected changes are within this range). SSP = shared socioeconomic pathway.

NOTES

1. The seminal and classic study is Wade 1982. More recent examples include Rinaudo 2002 and Rijsberman 2008.
2. At the same time, evidence from the Middle East presented in *Ebb and Flow: Volume 2* (Borgomeo et al. 2021) suggests that risks associated with water in particular are more often associated with cooperation than with conflict. This is because long-term exposure to water scarcity can strengthen water users' preference for cooperation.
3. The "big push" model in development economics was first developed by Paul Rosenstein-Rodan (1961). It conjectures that an economy may be stuck at a low-level equilibrium, where a lack of demand prevents firms from making investments to improve productivity. Small, piece-by-piece investments might not be enough to spur demand and instead a *big push*, whereby entire industries are transformed, is needed to jump-start self-sustaining growth and push the economy to a more productive equilibrium.

REFERENCES

Acemoglu, D., L. Fergusson, and S. Johnson. 2020. "Population and Conflict." *Review of Economic Studies* 87 (4): 1565–604.

Almazroui, M., F. Saeed, S. Saeed, M. N. Islam, M. Ismail, N. A. B. Klutse, and M. H. Siddiqui. 2020. Projected Change in Temperature and Precipitation over Africa from CMIP6. *Earth Systems and Environment* 4 (3): 455–75.

Almond, D., and J. Currie. 2011. "Killing Me Softly: The Fetal Origins Hypothesis." *Journal of Economic Perspectives* 25 (3): 153–72.

Angelsen, A., P. Jagger, R. Babigumira, B. Belcher, N. J. Hogarth, S. Bauch, J. Börner, C. Smith-Hall, and S. Wunder. 2014. "Environmental Income and Rural Livelihoods: A Global-Comparative Analysis." *World Development* 64 (Suppl. 1): S12–28.

Benami, E., Z. Jin, M. R. Carter, A. Ghosh, R. J. Hijmans, A. Hobbs, B. Kenduiywo, and D. B. Lobell. 2021. "Uniting Remote Sensing, Crop Modelling and Economics for Agricultural Risk Management." *Nature Reviews Earth & Environment* 2: 140–59.

Borgomeo, E., M. Mortazavi-Naeini, J. W. Hall, and B. P. Guillod. 2018. "Risk, Robustness and Water Resources Planning under Uncertainty." *Earth's Future* 6 (3): 468–87.

Borgomeo, Edoardo, Anders Jägerskog, Esha Zaveri, Jason Russ, Amjad Khan, and Richard Damania. 2021. *Ebb and Flow: Volume 2. Water in the Shadow of Conflict in the Middle East and North Africa.* Washington, DC: World Bank.

Browder, G., A. Nunez Sanchez, B. Jongman, N. Engle, E. van Beek, M. Castera Errea, and S. Hodgson. 2021. *An EPIC Response: Innovative Governance for Flood and Drought Risk Management.* Washington, DC: World Bank.

Burke, M., and V. Tanutama. 2019. "Climatic Constraints on Aggregate Economic Output." Working Paper 25779, National Bureau of Economic Research, Cambridge, MA.

Cattaneo, C., and G. Peri. 2016. "The Migration Response to Increasing Temperatures." *Journal of Development Economics* 122: 127–46.

Chambwera, M., G. Heal, C. Dubeux, S. Hallegatte, L. Leclerc, A. Markandya, B. A. McCarl, R. Mechler, and J. E. Neumann. 2014. "Economics of Adaptation." In *Climate Change 2014: Impacts, Adaptation, and Vulnerability. Part A: Global and Sectoral Aspects. Contribution of Working Group II to the Fifth Assessment Report of the Intergovernmental Panel on Climate Change*, edited by C. B. Field, V. R. Barros, D. J. Dokken, K. J. Mach, M. D. Mastrandrea, T. E. Bilir, M. Chatterjee, K. L. Ebi, Y. O. Estrada, R. C. Genova, B. Girma, E. S. Kissel, A. N. Levy, S. MacCracken. P. R. Mastrandrea, and L. L. White, 945–77. Cambridge, UK, and New York: Cambridge University Press.

Chan, F. K., J. Griffiths, E. Higgitt, S. Xu, F. Zhu, Y. T. Tang, Y. Xu, and C. Thorne. 2018. "'Sponge City' in China: A Breakthrough of Planning and Flood Risk Management in the Urban Context." *Land Use Policy* 76: 772–78.

Clemens, M., and M. Mendola. 2020. "Migration from Developing Countries: Selection, Income Elasticity, and Simpson's Paradox." CGD Working Paper 538, Center for Global Development, Washington, DC.

Collier, P. 2013. *Exodus: How Migration Is Changing Our World.* Oxford, UK: Oxford University Press.

Damania, R., A. Joshi, and J. Russ. 2020. "India's Forests: Stepping Stone or Millstone for the Poor?" *World Development* 125: 104451.

Ehrlich, I., and G. S. Becker. 1972. "Market Insurance, Self-Insurance, and Self-Protection." *Journal of Political Economy* 80 (4): 623–48.

Fankhauser, S. 2017. "Adaptation to Climate Change." *Annual Review of Resource Economics* 9: 209–30.

Flörke, M., C. Schneider, and R. I. McDonald. 2018. "Water Competition between Cities and Agriculture Driven by Climate Change and Urban Growth." *Nature Sustainability* 1 (1): 51–58.

Garrick, D., L. De Stefano, W. Yu, I. Jorgensen, E. O'Donnell, L. Turley, I. Aguilar-Barajas, X. Dai, R. de Souza Leão, B. Punjabi, B. Schreiner, J. Svensson, and C. Wight. 2019. "Rural Water for Thirsty Cities: A Systematic Review of Water Reallocation from Rural to Urban Regions." *Environmental Research Letters* 14 (4): 043003.

Glaeser, E. L. 2005. "Should the Government Rebuild New Orleans, or Just Give Residents Checks?" *Economists' Voice* 2 (4): art. 4.

Gray, C., and V. Mueller. 2012. "Natural Disasters and Population Mobility in Bangladesh." *Proceedings of the National Academy of Sciences* 109 (16): 6000–6005.

Groves, D. G., L. Bonzanigo, J. Syme, N. L. Engle, and I. Rodriguez Cabanillas. 2019. "Preparing for Future Droughts in Lima, Peru: Enhancing Lima's Drought Management Plan to Meet Future Challenges." World Bank, Washington, DC.

Guannel, G., K. Arkema, P. Ruggiero, and G. Vertues. 2016. "The Power of Three: Coral Reefs, Seagrasses and Mangroves Protect Coastal Regions and Increase Their Resilience." *PLoS One* 11 (7): e0158094.

Hallegatte, S., A. Shah, C. Brown, R. Lempert, and S. Gill. 2012. "Investment Decision Making under Deep Uncertainty—Application to Climate Change." World Bank Policy Research Working Paper 6193, World Bank, Washington, DC.

Hansen, Z. K., G. D. Libecap, and S. E. Lowe. 2011. "Climate Variability and Water Infrastructure: Historical Experience in the Western United States." In *The Economics of Climate Change: Adaptations Past and Present*, edited by G. D. Libecap and R. H. Steckel, 253–80. Chicago: University of Chicago Press.

Harari, M., and E. L. Ferrara. 2018. "Conflict, Climate, and Cells: A Disaggregated Analysis." *Review of Economics and Statistics* 100 (4): 594–608.

Hornbeck, R., and P. Keskin. 2014. "The Historically Evolving Impact of the Ogallala Aquifer: Agricultural Adaptation to Groundwater and Drought." *American Economic Journal: Applied Economics* 6 (1): 190–219.

Hyland, M., and J. Russ. 2019. "Water as Destiny: The Long-Term Impacts of Drought in Sub-Saharan Africa." *World Development* 115: 30–45.

James, R., and R. Washington. 2013. "Changes in African Temperature and Precipitation Associated with Degrees of Global Warming." *Climatic Change* 117 (4): 859–72.

Kapoor, P. 2021. "An Investment Planning Tool for Green Cities." *Sustainable Cities* (blog), January 19. https://blogs.worldbank.org/sustainablecities/investment-planning-tool-green-cities.

Khan, A. and A.-S. Rodella. Forthcoming. "A Hard Rain's a-Gonna Fall: New Insights on Water Security and Fragility in the Sahel." Washington, DC: World Bank.

Kocornik-Mina, A., T. K. McDermott, G. Michaels, and F. Rauch. 2020. "Flooded Cities." *American Economic Journal: Applied Economics* 12 (2): 35–66.

Lall, S.V., and U. Deichmann. 2010. *Density and Disasters: Economics of Urban Hazard Risk*. Washington, DC: World Bank.

Lall, S., W. Maloney, and A. Grover. 2021. *Place, Productivity, and Prosperity: Revisiting Spatially Targeted Policies for Regional Development.* Washington, DC: World Bank.

Lall, S.V., C. Timmins, and S. Yu. 2009. "Connecting Lagging and Leading Regions: The Role of Labor Mobility." Policy Research Working Paper 4843, World Bank, Washington, DC.

Maccini, S., and D. Yang. 2009. "Under the Weather: Health, Schooling, and Economic Consequences of Early-Life Rainfall." *American Economic Review* 99 (3): 1006–26.

McGuirk, E. F., and N. Nunn. 2020. *Nomadic Pastoralism, Climate Change, and Conflict in Africa.* Cambridge, MA: National Bureau of Economic Research.

Miguel, E., S. Satyanath, and E. Sergenti. 2004. "Economic Shocks and Civil Conflict: An Instrumental Variables Approach." *Journal of Political Economy* 112 (4): 725–53.

Monchuk, V. 2013. *Reducing Poverty and Investing in People: The New Role of Safety Nets in Africa.* Washington, DC: World Bank.

Niang, I., O.C. Ruppel, M.A. Abdrabo, A. Essel, C. Lennard, J. Padgham, and P. Urquhart. 2014. "Africa." In *Climate Change 2014: Impacts, Adaptation, and Vulnerability. Part B: Regional Aspects. Contribution of Working Group II to the Fifth Assessment Report of the Intergovernmental Panel on Climate Change*, edited by V. R. Barros, C. B. Field, D. J. Dokken, M. D. Mastrandrea, K. J. Mach, T. E. Bilir, M. Chatterjee, K. L. Ebi, Y. O. Estrada, R. C. Genova, B. Girma, E. S. Kissel, A. N. Levy, S. MacCracken, P. R. Mastrandrea, and L. L. White, 1199–265. Cambridge, UK, and New York: Cambridge University Press.

Ortiz-Bobea, A., T. R. Ault, C. M. Carrillo, R. G. Chambers, and D. B. Lobell. 2021. "Anthropogenic Climate Change Has Slowed Global Agricultural Productivity Growth." *Nature Climate Change* 11 (4): 306–12.

Peri, G., and A. Sasahara. 2019. "The Impact of Global Warming on Rural-Urban Migrations: Evidence from Global Big Data." Working Paper 25728, National Bureau of Economic Research, Cambridge, MA.

Rijsberman, F. R. 2008. "Water for Food: Corruption in Irrigation Systems." In *Global Corruption Report 2008: Corruption in the Water Sector*, 67. Berlin: Transparency International.

Rinaudo, J. D. 2002. "Corruption and Allocation of Water: The Case of Public Irrigation in Pakistan." *Water Policy* 4 (5): 405–22.

Rosenstein-Rodan, P.N. 1961. "Notes on the Theory of the 'Big Push.'" In *Economic Development for Latin America*, edited by H.S. Ellis and H. C. Wallich, 57–81. International Economic Association Series. London: Palgrave Macmillan. https://doi.org/10.1007/978-1-349-08449-4_3.

Rosenzweig, M. R., and C. R. Udry. 2019. "Assessing the Benefits of Long-Run Weather Forecasting for the Rural Poor: Farmer Investments and Worker Migration in a Dynamic Equilibrium Model." NBER Working Paper 25894, National Bureau of Economic Research, Cambridge, MA.

Siebert, S., M. Kummu, M. Porkka, P. Döll, N. Ramankutty, and B. R. Scanlon. 2015. "A Global Data Set of the Extent of Irrigated Land from 1900 to 2005." *Hydrology and Earth System Sciences* 19 (3): 1521–45.

Singh, C., G. Jain, V. Sukhwani, and R. Shaw. 2021. "Losses and Damages Associated with Slow-Onset Events: Urban Drought and Water Insecurity in Asia." *Current Opinion in Environmental Sustainability* 50: 72–86.

Varadhan, S. 2019. "Villagers Accuse City of Seizing Water as Drought Parches 'India's Detroit.'" Reuters, July 3.

Wade, R. 1982. "The System of Administrative and Political Corruption: Canal Irrigation in South India." *Journal of Development Studies* 18 (3): 287–328.

World Bank. 2015. *South Asia—Investment Decision Making in Hydropower: Decision Tree Case Study of the Upper Arun Hydropower Project and Koshi Basin Hydropower Development in Nepal* (English). Washington, DC: World Bank Group.

World Bank. 2018a. *Building the Resilience of Water Supply and Sanitation Utilities to Climate Change and Other Threats: A Roadmap.* Washington, DC: World Bank.

World Bank. 2018b. *Sahel Adaptive Social Protection Program: Addressing the Challenges of Climate Change and Disaster Risk for the Poor and Vulnerable.* Washington, DC: World Bank. http://documents.worldbank.org/curated /en/973501518153667496/Sahel-adaptive-social-protection-program -addressing-the-challenges-of-climate-change-and-disaster-risk-for-the-poor -and-vulnerable.

World Bank. 2020. "Resilient Water Infrastructure Design Brief." World Bank, Washington, DC.

World Bank. 2021. *Global Economic Prospects, January 2021.* Washington, DC: World Bank. doi:10.1596/978-1-4648-1612-3.

World Bank and International Energy Agency. 2015. *Progress toward Sustainable Energy for All 2015.* Washington, DC: World Bank.

Zaveri, E., D. S. Grogan, K. Fisher-Vanden, S. Frolking, R. B. Lammers, D. H. Wrenn, A. Prusevich, and R. E. Nicholas. 2016. "Invisible Water, Visible Impact: Groundwater Use and Indian Agriculture Under Climate Change." *Environmental Research Letters* 11 (8): 084005.